Learning to Counsel

If you want to know how...

Thrive on Stress
Manage pressure and positively thrive on it

365 Steps to Self-Confidence
A programme for personal transformation in just a few minutes a day

Trust Your Intuition
Harness the wisdom and power of your inner voice

Feeling Good
Proven tools for lifelong happiness

Please send for a free copy of the latest catalogue:

howtobooks

How To Books
3 Newtec Place, Magdalen Road,
Oxford OX4 1RE, United Kingdom
email: info@howtobooks.co.uk
http://www.howtobooks.co.uk

Learning
to Counsel

Second edition

Jan Sutton & William Stewart

howtobooks

Published in 2002 by
How To Books Ltd, 3 Newtec Place,
Magdalen Road, Oxford, OX4 1RE, United Kingdom.
Tel: (01865) 798306. Fax: (01865) 248780.
email: info@howtobooks.co.uk
http://www.howtobooks.co.uk

First edition 1997
Reprinted 1998
Second edition 2002
Reprinted 2003
Reprinted 2004 (twice)

British Library Cataloguing in Publication Data
A catalogue record for this book is available from
the British Library

Cover design by Baseline Arts Ltd.

Produced for How To Books by Deer Park Productions
Typeset by PDQ Typesetting, Newcastle-under-Lyme
Printed and bound by Bell & Bain Ltd, Glasgow

Note: The material contained in this book is set out in good
faith for general guidance and no liability can be accepted for
loss or expenses incurred as a result of relying in particular
circumstances on statements made in the book. The laws and
regulations are complex and liable to change, and readers
should check the current position with the relevant
authorities before making personal arrangements.

Contents

Foreword

The new edition of this excellent and user-friendly book is comprehensive and easy to read and comes alive with illustrative graphics and quotations. It is ideal for new and mature students in counselling and explains the core skills, conditions and models of counselling used in the UK.

The book is compelling reading for the student of counselling who is serious about self-reflection and personal development. Its practical approach is both exciting and refreshing and enables the reader to quickly understand and apply key counselling concepts, models and skills. In this way it helps the student or counselling practitioner keep up to date with current thought and models of counselling.

I would certainly recommend this enhanced second edition as an excellent resource for counselling courses and programmes.

Neil Morrison
Director of Institute of Counselling, Dixon Street Glasgow

Preface

Being invited to produce a second edition of what has proved a popular book is very satisfying, and writing it has been an exciting and rewarding experience for both of us. Since publication of the first edition, we have been greatly encouraged by the positive feedback received from students of counselling and tutors alike.

At the time of writing the first edition, the book was based on our experiences of running counselling workshops and lecturing. Now, with numerous published books between us, more knowledge of various aspects of counselling, and insight gained from a supervision group which we share in jointly with two other experienced colleagues, our learning has increased considerably and we hope this is reflected in this new edition.

We have gone through the first edition with a fine tooth-comb, removing several sections which, with the benefit of hindsight, now seem irrelevant. Most chapters have been reworked, updated, and new sections and additional examples have been added. Many of the original illustrations have been modified to improve clarity and consistency, and three new diagrams have been incorporated to enhance learning. The glossary, useful organisations, and further reading sections have been extensively developed and updated. These additions, plus a new and wide-ranging section of informative websites, provide the reader with an invaluable resource, thus adding a new dimension to the book. Finally, to add a touch of warmth, some inspirational quotes have been added to the chapters.

Written in an easy reading style, this practical book will be of particular interest to anyone considering a career in counselling. With its wealth of case studies, examples of skills, illustrations, and exercises, it will also be a valuable tool for tutors of counselling skills courses. Additionally, it will benefit those who use counselling skills as part of their work: for example, mental health workers, alternative therapists, volunteer counsellors, teachers, managers, doctors, nurses, probation officers, social workers, personnel officers, trainers and tutors, ministers, residential workers, community workers and pastoral care workers. Indeed, it is our belief that the skill presented here can enhance all human relationships.

The framework of the book is based firmly in the person-centred approach of Carl Rogers, and the skills-based approach of Gerard Egan. Carl Rogers suggested that if counsellors can plant the core conditions necessary for growth – genuineness, unconditional positive regard, and empathic understanding – these enable a healthy and nurturing relationship between counsellor and client to flourish. He believed that these conditions were sufficient to bring about growth and change in clients, enabling them to move towards fulfilment of their own potential.

Gerard Egan suggested that in addition to providing the core conditions, counsellors may need to help clients make decisions, clarify and set goals, and to support them with implementing their action. In his three-stage model, Egan analyses the skills which the counsellor needs to develop and use for each stage of the model.

To become a professional counsellor takes years of training and supervised counselling practice, and we would not presume to suggest that by reading this book you will have at your fingertips all that it takes to become an effective counsellor. A knowledge and understanding of the major theories of counselling is important. However, counsellors can benefit from a model to guide them in their work, together with a repertoire of skills, and a careful study of the principles outlined here will provide a basis for counselling practice.

The book has been arranged in a logical sequence and we recommend that you work through the case studies and exercises in the sequence presented. **Please ensure you have a pen and notebook handy to write down your responses to the exercises.** Throughout most of the chapters we follow five fictional clients to demonstrate the skills.

We hope this new edition will provide you with some understanding of what is involved in counselling; will help you achieve some insight and appreciation of counselling, and will help you develop the skills you need to counsel more effectively.

To avoid the clumsy formula of he/she we have used them interchangeably throughout the book.

Finally, we would like to thank Giles Lewis, Nikki Read and Regina Schinner at How To Books, for their continued support for our work. Also, our appreciation goes to Neil Morrison for writing the foreword.

Jan Sutton
William Stewart

CHAPTER 1

Defining Counselling

Counselling takes place when a counsellor sees a client in a private and confidential setting to explore a difficulty the client is having, distress they may be experiencing or perhaps their dissatisfaction with life, or loss of a sense of direction and purpose. It is always at the request of the client as no one can properly be 'sent' for counselling. (BACP, What is Counselling?)

It could be said that the general aim of counselling is to increase the client's self-awareness and insights and to marshal these new-found strengths in working towards an action plan that will help him cope more effectively with life (Stewart, 1983).

The aim of this chapter is to clarify what counselling is and is not, to develop understanding regarding the limits of confidentiality, explore what defines a 'counsellor', and identify the three basic elements involved in learning to counsel effectively – knowledge and understanding, developing skills, and personal development.

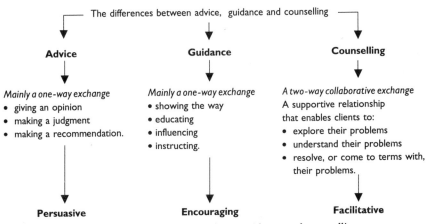

Fig. 1. The differences between advice, guidance and counselling.

What is counselling?

> *Give help rather than advice.*
>
> Marquis De Vauvenargues

The dictionary defines counselling as advice or guidance, yet the word 'advice' is an anathema to many counsellors. Figure 1 clarifies the differences.

Clarifying why counselling is not advice-giving

*Advice frequently means telling people what they should do or ought to do, and this has no place in counselling. Counsellors help clients look at what is *possible*, but do not tell clients what they should do. That would be the counsellor *taking control* rather than the client *gaining* control.

The counsellor who answers the question 'What would you advise me to do?' with 'What ideas have you had?' is helping the client to recognise that they have a part to play in seeking an answer. They help the client take responsibility for finding a solution that feels right for them.

Advice is often appropriate in crises; at times when a person's thoughts and feelings seem shocked by an event. At times like these the counsellor will exercise greater caution than when clients are fully responsive and responsible. Advice offered and accepted when in crisis, and then acted upon, could prove to be, if not 'bad advice', not totally appropriate to meet the client's needs. When people are under **stress** they are vulnerable. For all these reasons, counsellors are wary about responding to a request for advice.

However, it is sometimes very difficult not to offer advice. If a client is stressed, for example, the counsellor may suggest relaxation techniques to help reduce stress levels. Even though the advice might be 'good', the choice should always remain with the client.

Examining why counselling is not persuasion

Counselling is not persuading, prevailing upon, overcoming the client's resistances, wearing the client down or 'bringing the client to their senses'. Persuasion is in direct conflict with at least one principle of counselling, self-direction – the client's right to choose for themselves their course of action. If the counsellor were to persuade the client to go a certain way, make a certain choice, there could be a very real danger of the whole affair backfiring in the counsellor's face and resulting in further damage to the client's self-esteem.

This concept of self-direction, based on personal freedom, is the touchstone of the non-directive approach to counselling but is present in most others. The basis of the principle is that:

◆ any pressure which is brought to bear on the client will increase conflict and so hamper exploration.

Exploring why counselling is not exercising undue influence

Some people believe that successful counsellors are those who are able to suggest solutions to clients' problems in such a way that the clients feel they are their own. This is commonly called 'manipulation', behaviour from which most counsellors would recoil. However, situations are seldom clear cut. There is a fine line between legitimate influence and manipulation. Manipulation always carries with it some benefit to the manipulator. Influence is generally unconscious. In any case, suggesting solutions is not part of effective counselling. There is a difference between exploring alternatives and suggesting solutions and manipulation. Manipulation invariably leaves the person on the receiving end feeling uncomfortable, used and angry.

The dividing line between manipulation and seeking ways and means to resolve a problem may not always be easily seen, but the deciding factor must be *who benefits?* Is it you, or is the other person?

(*Adapted from *Going for Counselling*, William Stewart and Angela Martin (How To Books, 1999) and used by permission of the authors.)

Identifying the difference between counselling and other forms of helping

> *Nature gave us one tongue and two ears so we could hear twice as much as we speak.*
>
> Epictetus

The primary difference between counselling and other forms of helping is the way in which the counsellor listens. Active listening is at the heart of effective counselling. Active listening involves listening at a 'head' level to the thinking behind the client's words, and at a 'heart' level to the feelings and emotions behind them. It also entails being aware of (a form of listening) the client's non-verbal communication – eye contact, eye movements, tone of voice (harsh or soft), gestures (sighing, clenching fists), body posture (slumped, tense, open, closed), facial expressions (smiling, frowing), mannerisms, and mode of dress (smart, casual). Non-verbal communication, or body language as it is commonly called, can provide the counsellor with significant information about what the client may not be expressing but may be feeling

Is there a dividing line between counselling and other forms of helping?

We go to a doctor when we have something medically wrong; to a psychiatrist when there is something mentally wrong; to a priest when there is something spiritually wrong. All of these establish a helping relationship; but what they offer is not counselling, not in the sense we mean in this book. However, these three professionals may also use counselling skills; they may also be trained counsellors. So the dividing line is not clear cut.

When a doctor is diagnosing and prescribing, he is not counselling. The principal difference is that the person knows when counselling is taking place and has agreed to it. In other words, a counselling contract is established (see Chapter 3 for an example of a counselling contract and further discussion on the topic).

What defines a 'counsellor'?

As discussed above, not every person who uses counselling skills is designated a 'counsellor'. We can distinguish two broad groups of people who use counselling skills: people who are called 'counsellors', who engage in counselling as a distinct occupation, and others who use counselling skills as part of their other skills. They would be temporarily in the role.

Understanding confidentiality

Counsellors are frequently the observers, and often the recipients, of confidential material about clients, their life situations and intimate details of their families. Confidentiality, at first glance, is deceptively simple. It means not disclosing secret details about another person which have been disclosed during counselling.

It is helpful to distinguish between *secret* and *confidential* material. Everything said in a counselling interview is confidential, but not everything is a secret. The belief that absolutely everything the client says must never be shared with anyone can lead to problems.

Consider the case of the man who admits that he has been stealing from the organisation in which you both work. Should this information be passed on and to whom? If you become party to information which you feel must be passed on, you ought to explain to the client why and to whom you must pass it.

Professional counsellors are bound by certain ethics, which are not applicable in their totality to people using counselling skills as part of their repertoire of work skills. *Feelings* as well as *facts* should not be shared indiscriminately.

The limits of confidentiality

Confidentiality is limited by:
- Whose needs predominate?
- Who would be harmed?
- Do the needs of the agency have to be considered?
- The laws of the land.
- Do the needs of the wider society have to be considered?
- Who might be placed at risk?

Individual counsellors need to be quite clear what information, gleaned through counselling, they may pass on and to whom. Some clients need to be reassured of confidentiality. Counsellors should take time to clarify precisely what the client understands by confidentiality.

> *The person's right to secrecy is never absolute. Counsellors may be required by a court to pass on secret information. Failure to do so may involve imprisonment for contempt of court.*

An example of selective confidentiality

Carlos was being admitted to hospital for surgery. During the course of the assessment interview he revealed that he had a criminal record. The nurse decided that this information, if withheld, would not affect the treatment. She did not include this detail in the notes, but concentrated on Carlos' anxiety about his forthcoming exploratory operation for cancer.

Learning to counsel

There are three basic elements involved in learning to counsel effectively:

1. **Knowledge and understanding.** This involves:
   - gaining knowledge of the theory of personality development underlying the counselling approach used and
   - gaining knowledge of common psychological processes, for example bereavement and loss and relationship interactions.

2. **Developing skills.** This involves:
   - changing behaviour, which can feel very uncomfortable to begin with. However, in time, and with practice, the skills feel more comfortable and you start to use them without even thinking about them – they become part of your style.

3. **Personal development.** This involves:
   - being able to separate your own feelings from those of the client. This means increasing self-awareness: the more self-awareness gained, the more you are able to understand your clients.

The primary focus of this book is on two of the elements involved in learning to counsel effectively:
- ◆ skills development
- ◆ personal development.

Summary

In this chapter we have established the aims of counselling, clarified what counselling is and is not, examined the limits of confidentiality within the counselling relationship, explained what defines a 'counsellor', and pinpointed three basic elements required to counsel effectively. We have demonstrated that:

- ◆ The primary difference between counselling and other forms of helping is the way in which the counsellor listens.
- ◆ Everything said in a counselling interview is confidential, but not everything is secret.
- ◆ There are three basic elements involved in counselling training:
  1. knowledge of counselling theory
  2. skills development
  3. personal development.

> *Advice is seldom welcome; and those*
> *who want it the most always like it the least.*
> Philip Dormer Stanhope (fourth Earl of Chesterfield)

CHAPTER 2

Exploring Essential Counsellor Qualities

As we grow as unique persons, we learn to respect the uniqueness of others.

Robert H. Schulle

Having established the aims of counselling, and identified what counselling is and is not, we move on to examine three counsellor qualities or attitudes considered by Carl Rogers as vital for therapeutic change: **genuineness, unconditional regard** and **empathic understanding**. Also referred to as the core conditions, these qualities are essential to building a therapeutic alliance (a collaborative client-counsellor relationship – strong bond – growth-promoting environment). These key characteristics are summarised in Figure 2.

Essential counsellor qualities 'the core conditions'

Genuineness   Unconditional positive regard   Empathic understanding

Aim: to build a therapeutic alliance.

Fig. 2. Essential counsellor qualities.

Developing self-awareness is also a crucial aspect in the personal development of a counsellor. In this and subsequent chapters, exercises designed to increase your self-awareness are included, so make sure you have a notebook handy from here on.

Elaborating on essential counsellor qualities

Fundamentally, the counsellor qualities mentioned are relationship qualities that are embraced in most therapies, and deemed crucial in person-centred counselling. Briefly, they include the counsellor's ability to:

♦ **demonstrate genuineness:** being oneself (open, transparent) in the relationship, not hiding behind a mask of professionalism (also known as congruence, realness or authenticity)

♦ **show unconditional positive regard:** acceptance of the client without judgment or conditions attached (also referred to as caring, valuing, prizing, respect)

♦ **convey a deep level of empathic understanding:** the ability to step into the client's world – *as if* you are in their shoes and without losing the *as if* quality.

We will take a closer look at the qualities outlined above.

Genuineness

This is the degree to which we are freely and deeply ourselves, and are able to relate to people in a sincere and non-defensive manner. For example, we may not approve of an aspect of the client's behaviour, and may aim to find a way to sensitively point this out to the client. Genuineness is the precondition for empathy and unconditional positive regard. Effective counselling depends wholly on the degree to which the counsellor is integrated and genuine.

Genuineness encourages client self-disclosure. Appropriate counsellor disclosure enhances genuineness. The genuine counsellor does not feel under any compulsion to disclose, either about events, situations, or feelings aroused within the counselling relationship.

Showing non-possessive warmth

Non-possessive warmth is genuine. It springs from an attitude of friendliness towards others. A relationship in which friendliness is absent will not flourish. Showing non-possessive warmth makes the client feel comfortable. It is liberating, non-demanding, and melts the coldness and hardness within people's hearts.

Conveying warmth

We convey warmth by:

- body language – posture, proximity, personal space, facial expressions, eye contact
- words and the way we speak: tone of voice, delivery, rate of speech
- all the indicators of warmth – the non-verbal parts of speech and body language must be in agreement with the words used; any discrepancy between the words and how we deliver them will cause confusion in the other person.

Warmth, like a hot water bottle, must be used with great care. Someone who is very cold, distant, cynical, mistrustful, could feel very threatened by someone else's depth of warmth. A useful analogy would be to think how an iceberg would react in the presence of sun.

Unconditional positive regard

Unconditional positive regard is about valuing and respecting the client as a unique human being. It's about conveying a non-possessive caring and acceptance of the client, irrespective of how offensive the client's behaviour might be. Demonstrating unconditional positive regard facilitates change. It is where we communicate a deep and genuine caring, not filtered through our own feelings, thoughts and behaviours. **Conditional regard** implies enforced control, and compliance with behaviour dictated by someone else.

Demonstrating acceptance

Inherent in the idea of demonstrating acceptance is that the counsellor does not judge the client by some set of rules or standards. This means that counsellors have to be able to suspend their own judgments. Acceptance is a special kind of loving which moves out toward people as they are, and maintains their dignity and personal worth. It means accepting their strengths and weaknesses; their favourable and unfavourable qualities; their positive and negative attitudes; their constructive and destructive wishes, and their thoughts, feelings, and behaviours.

Understanding what acceptance means

Communicating acceptance means we avoid pressurising the client to become someone else, we do not take control, and we avoid being judgmental, critical, or condemning. We do not attach 'if' clauses; eg 'I will love you if…'. Clients will test the counsellor's unconditional acceptance, until they sense that the counsellor accepts them as they are, without approval or disapproval, and without making the client feel less of a person.

When counsellors accept clients just as they are, clients accept counsellors just as they are, with *their* strengths and weaknesses, with their successes and failures. The degree to which we accept other people is dependent on the degree of our own self-awareness. Only if we are well grounded psychologically can we work with other people to mobilise their feelings and energies toward change, growth and fulfilment.

When we feel accepted as we truly are, including our strengths and weaknesses and differences of opinions, no matter how unpleasant or uncongenial, we feel liberated from many of the things that enslave us.

Acceptance is client-centred

Acceptance is directed to the needs of the client, rather than to the counsellor's own needs. Acceptance recognises the potential of the client for self-help, and it encourages the promotion of growth of the client. Acceptance contains elements of the counsellor's thoughts (knowledge, psychological grounding), feelings (use of self), and behaviour (which must be congruent with what we say).

The qualities of acceptance

◆ caring
◆ concern
◆ compassion
◆ consistency
◆ courtesy
◆ firmness
◆ interest

- ◆ listening
- ◆ moving toward
- ◆ prizing
- ◆ respect
- ◆ valuing
- ◆ warmth.

Obstacles to acceptance

There are numerous obstacles that can get in the way of acceptance. One major stumbling block is **stereotyping**.

Stereotyping explained

Stereotyping, also described as labelling, classifying, typecasting, pigeon-holing, categorising, putting in a mould, pre-judging or making assumptions, is our beliefs about people or groups of people. For example, if we say something like, '*Well let's face it, what can you expect... they're all the same*' we are stereotyping. Referring to someone as a 'dumb blonde', or 'fiery redhead' are other forms. Stereotyping allows no room for individuality, and is generally negative. It stems from our deeply embedded and often conditioned conviction about others, and may be due to fear or a lack of understanding about people different to ourselves. Minority groups are often the butt of stereotyping, for instance: gays, alcoholics, drug addicts, stammerers, the mentally ill, the disabled, the hard of hearing, the visually impaired, unmarried mothers, ethnic minorities, asylum seekers, smokers, self-injurers, students. It can also be aimed at people employed in specific occupations – social workers, police, priests, or those with a different accent – the list is endless.

Stereotyping can have a damaging effect on the therapeutic alliance. To remain neutral, and to prevent putting a barrier in the way, counsellors need to listen to themselves carefully for any signs of 'putting their client into a niche'. And what better time to start than the present. Stop reading for a moment and close your eyes. Try to capture any images, feelings or reactions you experienced on reading about the groups mentioned above. Be honest with yourself. Were you guilty of stereotyping? Make a note in your notebook of any groups you particularly struggled with to remind yourself that this is an area you need to be aware of.

Other stumbling blocks to acceptance

◆ Lack of knowledge of human behaviour.
◆ Blocks or blind spots within self, for example, conscious hidden agendas, or unconscious unresolved conflicts.
◆ Attributing one's feelings to the client.
◆ Biases and prejudices, values, beliefs.
◆ Unfounded reassurances, unwillingness to explore.
◆ Confusion between acceptance and approval.
◆ Loss of respect for the client.
◆ Over-identification with the client, which may be an unconscious blind spot, or a conscious hidden agenda.

Demonstrating a non-judgmental attitude

Being non-judgmental is yet another important facet of acceptance. Judgment is to do with law, blame, guilty or innocent, and punishment. Clients may engage in self-judgment and will need to work through this if healing is to take place. Although counsellors are entitled to hold their own values, these should not be imposed on the client, and the counsellor must strive not to make judgments about their clients.

Understanding judgmentalism

Judgmentalism takes no account of feelings. It is critical, and condemns others because of their conduct or supposed false beliefs, wrong motives, or character. Judgmentalism is arbitrary, without room for negotiation or understanding and is an evaluation and rejection of another person's worth. The result of judgmentalism is that it dims, divides and fragments relationships.

Judgmentalism seeks to elevate one person above another. Within it are the characteristics of self-exaltation, self-promotion and the determination to be first on every occasion.

Judgment often attacks the person rather than the behaviour. Judgmentalism creates massive blind spots in our relationships. We cannot counsel people effectively while we are judging and condemning them. When we are troubled we nee help, not judgment.

When we pass judgment upon others, if we examine ourselves, we will find that the very thing on which we pass judgment is also present within ourselves in one degree or another.

Detecting judgmentalism

Judgmentalism can often be detected by such words as:
◆ should
◆ ought
◆ must
◆ got to
◆ don't

and by such phrases as:
◆ in my opinion
◆ I think . . .
◆ this is what you should do.

Why counsellors should avoid being judgmental

Judgmentalism is moralistic. It is based on norms and values, warning, approval/disapproval, instruction, and induces inferiority. Judgmentalism evokes inhibition, guilt and distress It is often associated with authority, control, hierarchy, rules and regulations that impose standards of behaviour. Judgmentalism is the opposite of acceptance. Judgmentalism paralyses: acceptance affirms and encourages action.

A judgmental response has a tendency to indicate that the counsellor has made a judgment of relative goodness, appropriateness, effectiveness, rightness. In some way the counsellor implies, however grossly or subtly, what the client might or ought to do. The responses imply a personal moral standpoint, and involve a judgment (critical or approving) of others.

Being non-judgmental is a fundamental quality of the counselling relationship. Demonstrating a non-judgmental attitude is based on the firmly held belief that assigning guilt innocence, or the degree to which the client is responsible, or not, for causing the problem has no place in the counselling relationship.

Clients who are nurtured within a non-judgmental relationship learn not to pass judgment upon themselves. Within this relationship they find the courage and the strength to change.

Being non-judgmental

'Non-judgmental' does not mean being valueless or without standards. It does mean trying not to mould others to fit into our value systems. Our values may be right for us; they may be totally wrong for other people.

Being non-judgmental means recognising and understanding our own values and standards so that we can suspend them and minimise their influence on the way we respond to other people. Counsellors must remain true to their own values and standards. They are not human chameleons. Whenever we speak, we communicate the unspoken judgment that lurks within our hearts.

When we feel non-judgmental, that feeling is communicated. No words can convey a non-judgmental attitude if it does not reside within the heart of the counsellor. Counsellors may not like all clients, but it is their duty to strive to be free from prejudices which will lead them into being judgmental. Being non-judgmental means holding within the heart respect for other people's opinions. Very often we are judgmental over trivial issues.

Developing a non-judgmental attitude

We can develop a non-judgmental attitude by:
- recognising and carefully scrutinising our own values and standards; we may decide to jettison some of them
- trying to see the world from the client's frame of reference
- not jumping to conclusions
- not saying, 'I know how you feel'
- not comparing the client to someone else
- not becoming over-involved.

To formulate a non-judgmental response involves:

◆ being receptive and accepting
◆ concentrating on what the client's experience means, not on the facts
◆ being interested in the person, not just in the problem itself
◆ demonstrating sincere respect for the client as a person of worth
◆ facilitating, not interpretreting unconscious motives
◆ trying to understand what it means to be this particular client
◆ getting into the client's inner world; their frame of reference
◆ not rushing to answer
◆ being aware of your own values
◆ hearing, then responding to, the client's expressed and implied feelings
◆ accepting that clients know more about their inner world than you do.

Empathic understanding

Empathic understanding is primarily a subjective experience on the part of the counsellor. It means having the ability to perceive the client's world as the client sees it – to grasp it from their frame of reference, and being able to communicate that understanding tentatively and sensitively. Demonstrating empathy means:

◆ being able to step into the client's shoes, and being able to step out again
◆ being able to stand back far enough to remain objective, rather than standing too close and risk becoming enmeshed in the client's world
◆ being close to, yet remaining separate from – it doesn't mean we become the other person.

Empathy works within the conditional framework of *as if* I were that other person. It taps into the listener's intuition and imagination.

Is there a difference between empathy, sympathy and pity?

Sympathy and pity are frequently confused with empathy, yet they are not the same. Sympathy could be defined as feeling *like*, or sharing in another's feelings, 'I know exactly how you must be feeling'. Pity, on the other hand, could be defined as feeling *for*, 'There, there, don't upset yourself so ... it hurts me to see you crying'. Whilst appropriate in certain situations, such as comforting someone who has recently experienced a bereavement, there is little room for sympathy and pity in counselling. Counselling is essentially about facilitating change. Expressing sympathy or pity can hinder this process by keeping the client stuck, or wallowing in their current situation. For empathy to mean anything, we have to respond in such a way that the other person feels that understanding has been reached, or is being striven for. It means constantly checking for inaccuracies, for example:

◆ 'Would I be right in thinking that...?'
◆ 'I think I understand what you mean ...but can I just recap to be sure.'
◆ 'What you seem to be saying is ... am I hearing you correctly?'

It means being *genuine* if we don't understand, for example:

◆ 'I'm not quite clear what you mean ... perhaps you could give me an example.'
◆ 'I'm getting a bit confused about...'
◆ 'I'm trying to get a picture of your situation but it's a bit fuzzy. I wonder if you would mind going over what you just said.'

Empathy is not a state that one reaches, nor a qualification that one is awarded. It is a transient thing. We can move in to it and lose it again very quickly. Literally, it means getting 'alongside'. Counsellors from a wide range of approaches rank empathy as being one of the highest qualities a counsellor can demonstrate.

Levels of empathy are related to the degree to which the client is able to explore and reach self-understanding. It can be taught within an empathic climate.

The three parts of empathy

1. **Thinking** (cognitive) – an intellectual or conceptual grasping of the feeling of another.

2. **Feeling** (affective) – a mirroring or sharing of the emotion with the other person.

3. **Behavioural** (doing) – assuming in one's mind the role of the other person.

Empathy is also communicated non-verbally through facial expression, eye contact, and a forward leaning of the trunk, and a reduction of the physical distance. Non-empathic body language weakens the spoken message, however deeply empathic it may be.

Empathy is not a gift from the gods, it is a skill we can all develop. Some might have to work very hard at it, for others it might come easily. If you find it difficult to pick out feelings and respond to them with empathy, try not to feel too discouraged. Keep plugging away at it, and find a sympathetic friend on whom you can practise.

Staying in the client's frame of reference

The frame of reference is a two-part concept which is emphasised in person-centred counselling. Figure 3 gives examples.

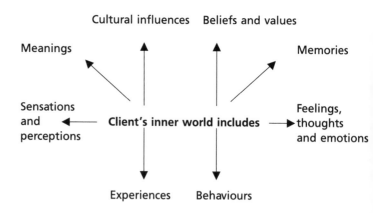

Fig. 3. Internal frame of reference (the inner world of the client).

External frame of reference: 'the inner world of the counsellor'

The contents of the counsellor's frame are similar to the
client's frame, and therein lies a danger. When the experiences
of one person are similar to someone else's, it is tempting to
'know' how the other person feels. This knowing cannot come
from our experience. It can only resonate within us as we listen
to what it means to the other person. The external frame of
reference is when we perceive only from our own subjective
frame of reference and when there is no accurate, empathic
understanding of the subjective world of the other person.

Evaluating another person through the values of our
external frame of reference will ensure lack of understanding.
When we view another person within the internal frame of
reference, that person's behaviour makes more sense. The
principal limitation is that we can then deal only with what is
within the consciousness of the other person. That which is
unconscious lies outside the frame of reference.

Building a bridge of empathy

For person A to understand the frame of reference of person B,
person A needs to build a bridge of empathy (see Figure 4) in
order to enter the person's world, help the other person
communicate, understand the personal meanings of B and to
communicate that understanding to B.

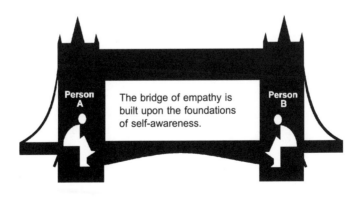

Fig. 4. Building a bridge of empathy.

Lack of self-awareness obstructs the ability to enter someone else's frame of reference. The more we feel able to express ourselves freely to another person, without feeling on trial, th more the contents of our frame of reference will be communicated.

Communicating with another person's frame of reference depends on:

1. Careful listening to the other person's total communicatio – words, non-verbal messages, voice-related cues.

2. Trying to identify the feelings that are being expressed, an behaviours that give rise to those feelings.

3. Trying to communicate an understanding of what the person seems to be feeling and of the sources of those feelings.

4. Responding by showing understanding, not by evaluating what has been said.

Gaining self-awareness

> *I want, by understanding myself, to understand others.*
> *I want to be all that I am capable of becoming.*
>
> Katherine Mansfie

To become effective counsellors, we need to constantly strive increase our self-awareness – to discover what makes us tick – to monitor what goes on inside our head: our thoughts, feelings, sensing, intuition, attitudes, beliefs, and how these manifest themselves in our behaviour. In other words, we nee to learn to 'read ourselves like a book' – the 'cover' and the 'contents'. Burnard (1997:25) defines self-awareness as '...the continuous and evolving process of getting to know who you are'. If we don't know 'who lives in here' and feel at home with ourselves, it's likely that our ability to help others will be impeded. A lack of self-knowledge means there are areas that are unknown or invisible to us. By increasing our self-understanding, we enhance our ability to be genuine and empathic, and our understanding of what makes other people tick.

Introducing the Johari Window

How do we become more self-aware?

The Johari Window (see Figure 5) helps us to understand ourselves. It is derived from the work of Jo Luft and Harry Ingram (1955) *The Johari Window: A Graphic Model for Interpersonal Relations,* University of California.

The self

1.
    Known to all
	2.
	    Blind

3.
    Hidden
	4.
	    Unknown to all

Fig. 5. Modified Johari Window.

Window 1 – Known to all

This part can be viewed as our open window. It is the parts of us that we freely display and other people see, for example our attitudes and behaviour. The open area of our window can be enlarged by self-disclosure.

Window 2 – Blind

This part can be viewed as the blind spots of our window. It is the parts of us that we cannot see but others can, for example our body language and other aspects of our behaviour that we are unaware of. The blind spots of our window can be enlarged by feedback from other people.

Window 3 – Hidden

This part can be viewed as the private part of our window. It is the parts of us that we know but choose not to share with others, for example our secrets or things we feel ashamed about. The hidden area of our window can be enlarged by taking risks, for example by disclosing our secrets.

Window 4 – Unknown to all

This part can be viewed as our closed window. It is the parts of us which we and others are unaware of. This part may include our motivations, unconscious needs, anxieties and undiscovered potential. The unknown part of our window can be enlarged through the counselling process by gradually opening up memories, and the gaining of insight.

Exercise

Exercise 1 – Expanding self-awareness (from your internal frame of reference)

You are advised not to rush through this exercise, for a greater understanding of your own frame of reference will aid your self-awareness and how what is within it may get in the way of entering a client's frame of reference. As this exercise is very individual, no answers will be provided.

1. **Name.**	How important is it to you?
2. **Gender.**	Are you satisfied with being who you are?
3. **Body.**	Are you satisfied with your physical appearance?
4. **Abilities.**	What are you particularly good at?
5. **Mind.**	Do you feel OK about your intellectual ability?
6. **Age.**	Are you comfortable with the age you are now?
7. **Birth.**	How do you feel about where you were born?
8. **Culture(s).**	Where were you brought up? If you have moved between different cultures, what influences has this had?
9. **People.**	Who influenced you most when growing up?
10. **Mother.**	What is your opinion of your mother?
11. **Father.**	What is your opinion of your father? If you have no parents, how has that influenced you?
12. **Siblings.**	What is your opinion of your brothers/sisters? If you have no brothers or sisters what influence has that had?

13. **Education.**	What influence did your education have? What would you like to have achieved but did not?
14. **Employment.**	List the various jobs you have had, the people you remember associated with those jobs, and the overall influence of the work and the associated people.
15. **Spouse.**	If you are married, how has your spouse influenced you?
16. **Children.**	How have your children influenced you? If you wanted children, and were unable to have them, how has that influenced you?
17. **Unmarried.**	If you are unmarried, or have no partner, what influence does that have?
18. **Preferences.**	How do your sexual preferences influence you?
19. **Values.**	What values do you have, and what influence do they exert? Have you taken them over from other people without thinking about them?
20. **Beliefs.**	What are your fundamental beliefs? How did you acquire them?
21. **Religion.**	If you are religious, what influence does that exert? If you have no religion, what influence does that exert?
22. **Experiences.**	What life experiences are significant for you, and why?
23. **Health.**	How have any illnesses or accidents influenced you?
24. **Memories.**	What memories do you treasure, and what memories do you try hard to forget?
25. **Relationships.**	What relationships in the past are you glad you had, and what relationships do you wish you had never had?
26. **Circumstances.**	What life circumstances, past or present, do you welcome, and which do you regret?
27. **Authority.**	Who represents authority for you, in the past and now? What influence do these authority figures exert on you?

28. **Strengths.**   What are your major strengths, and how might these influence your listening to clients?

29. **Weaknesses.**   What are your major weaknesses, and how might these influence your ability to listen to clients?

30. **Virtues.**   What do you consider to be your virtues? How do they influence your behaviour?

31. **Vices.**   Do you have any vices, and how do they influence your relationships?

How much insight do you think you gained by working through these 31 questions on your frame of reference?

Summary

The essential qualities required to be an effective counsellor are:

◆ the ability to be genuine with the client
◆ the ability to show non-possessive warmth towards the client
◆ the ability to show unconditional positive regard for the client
◆ the ability to show acceptance of the client (warts-and-all)
◆ the ability to suspend judgment of the client
◆ the ability to show empathic understanding to the client
◆ the ability to stay within the client's frame of reference
◆ the ability to take the risk of becoming more self-aware.

In this chapter we have introduced you to the counsellor qualities necessary to work effectively with others: genuineness, unconditional positive regard, and empathic understanding. We have also demonstrated the importance of gaining self-awareness. In Chapter 3, we look at what counsellors can do to help their clients feel safe so they can begin to explore their difficulties.

The first step to change is awareness.
The second step is acceptance.

Nathaniel Branden

A safe
environment is
crucial to
develop a strong
therapeutic
alliance.

CHAPTER 3

Helping the Client Feel Safe

Equality may perhaps be a right,
but no power on earth can ever turn it into a fact.

Honoré de Balzac

Seeking counselling takes courage, and it's natural for many
clients to feel apprehensive about the first meeting with the
counsellor. Creating a warm and safe physical environment is
an essential stepping-stone to building a strong therapeutic
alliance. In this chapter guidance is given on setting up the
counselling room in a way that helps the client feel comfortable
so that they start sharing their concerns. We also provide
examples of opening sentences to help break the ice, as well as
discussing some other important topics, including building
trust and boundary issues such as contracting and terminating
sessions on time.

Paying attention to meeting, greeting and seating

For counselling to be effective, the counsellor needs to work at
building a relationship of equals. This is easier said than done,
especially in the early stages when the client may be feeling
vulnerable and insecure, and bearing in mind that it is usual
for the client to meet the counsellor on unfamiliar territory, i.e.
the counsellor's consulting room. Striving to keep the room
neutral, in other words free from personal belongings such as
books, ornaments and family photographs, is a positive step
that counsellors can take to reduce the equality gap. Barriers
such as desks should also be avoided, and chairs should be
uniform and placed approximately three to four feet apart, and
slightly at an angle. Being in direct eye contact with the
counsellor can leave some clients feeling very uncomfortable or
embarrassed. A small clock needs to be positioned where the
counsellor can glance at it, and attention should be paid to the

lighting, and room temperature. A box of tissues strategically placed where the client can easily reach them is a must, and a vase of fresh flowers or a potted plant can add a touch of warmth and colour to the setting, and reflect something of your personality. With the client's permission, the counsellor may tape the sessions and this should be set up ready to use.

When meeting a new client, it is also important for the counsellor to pay attention to her own safety. Ensuring that someone else is around and having an alarm button close to hand can help to reduce any anxieties the counsellor might have. However, it should be pointed out that emotional barriers are far more potent that physical ones. Even if all the physical surroundings are perfect, the client still might not feel at ease if the counsellor and client are not in rapport. Figure 6 gives a view of how a counselling room might look.

Greeting the client

Greeting the client can be fairly informal:

1.   Hello Pat, I'm Jan. Please sit down (indicates chair).

2.   Hello Paul, my name is William. Please have a seat (indicates chair).

3.   Hello Mrs Williams, my name is Jan – what name would you like me to call you by?

4.   Hello, my name is William, and yours is?

Addressing clients by their first name can go a long way toward helping them feel comfortable and accepted. And introducing yourself by your first name can help to break down the barriers of unequality. However, do not assume that because you are feel comfortable being on first name terms that all people are. Ask the client how they want you to address them.

Issuing an open invitation to talk

Your opening sentence should be empathic and your posture should demonstrate to the client that you are ready to listen:

1.   Pat, perhaps you would like to tell me in your own time what has prompted you to come and see me?

2. Paul, we have about 50 minutes to talk together today. Where you would like to begin?

3. *To the confused client (Claire).* You seem to have a lot of concerns. Which one would it help to talk about first?

4. *To the reluctant client (Ellen).* I get the feeling that it's difficult for you to know where to begin.

5. *To the resistant client (Danny), who has been sent by a third party – eg magistrates.* I somehow sense that you don't really want to be here, and I'm wondering how you feel about being sent.

For examples of appropriate posture see Figure 11 (page 41).

Fig 6. A view of a how a counselling room might look.

Building trust

Some clients who seek counselling have been badly let down, hurt or abused by other people, and trust may therefore be a major issue. Trust is something that has to be earned by the counsellor and it can be hard work. However, developing the skills of active listening; accurate, sensitive responding; reflecting feelings; empathy; genuineness; and demonstrating that you are fully present for the client can help to establish a solid foundation of trust. Indeed, the more the counsellor invests in the relationship, the stronger the trust and bond grows between client and counsellor:

1. Pat, I can see that you are very distressed because of what has happened.

2. Paul, I appreciate that talking about your job being made redundant is very painful for you.

3. *To the confused client (Claire).* Claire, thank you for sharing your concerns with me.

4. *To the reluctant client (Ellen).* It's been brave of you to share so much with me.

5. *To the resistant client (Danny).* Thank you for being so honest by telling me how you feel about being here.

Knowing what to avoid

◆ Avoid restricting the client by placing emphasis on such topics as 'difficulties', 'problems', 'help'; for example, saying 'Please go ahead and tell me the problem'. 'What difficulties are you having?' 'How can I help you?' Be careful about statements such as 'I hope I can help you'. We may not be able to help at all.

◆ Avoid minimising counselling with expressions such as: 'Let's have a chat', or 'Shall we have a little talk?' Counselling is not a chat. We talk, yes, but 'chat' carries with it inferences of a social meeting, which is not the purpose of counselling. To think of it as chat demeans the process.

Establishing the ground rules for effective counselling

Establishing clear boundaries (the ground rules for counselling) is another important stepping stone to building the therapeutic alliance. Boundaries may include agreement over such things as the duration of counselling, length of counselling sessions, limits of confidentiality, appropriate touching, number and duration of phone calls, sending and responding to emails, or strategies for managing episodes of self-harm or suicidal thoughts.

The terms on which counselling is being offered should be made clear to clients before counselling commences. These may be agreed verbally, or they may be set out in a formal written contract between counsellor and client, and signed by both parties. Subsequent revision of these terms should be agreed in advance of any change. Clear contracting enhances, and shows respect for, the client's autonomy. A contract helps to ensure the professional nature of the relationship and may, in addition to the ground rules already mentioned, include:

◆ venue
◆ fees, if appropriate
◆ frequency of sessions
◆ how counselling will be evaluated
◆ process of referral, if and when necessary
◆ broad details of the counselling relationship
◆ duties and responsibilities of each party
◆ details of the counsellor's supervision
◆ goals of counselling
◆ means by which the goals will be achieved
◆ the provision and completion of 'homework'
◆ the setting of boundaries and expectations
◆ the terms of the therapeutic relationship
◆ provision for renegotiation of contract.

Gerard Egan, in the fourt edition of his popular book *The Skilled Helper* emphasises the point that:

> Ideally, the contract is an instrument that makes clients more informed about the process, more collaborative with their helpers, and more proactive in managing their problems. At its best, a contract can help client and helper

This contract is made between:

Counsellor: .... Client: ....

on the .... year ....

1. CONFIDENTIALITY

Although our sessions are confidential, I reserve the right to break confidentiality in the following circumstances:

i. As part of my ongoing training and personal development as a counsellor, I attend regular supervision sessions. During these sessions, I discuss my client work with my supervisor. However, to ensure confidentiality I will identify you by a code number only.

ii. If you provide me with information that appears to indicate an immediate threat to your own life or health, or to anyone else's, I reserve the right to report that information to your GP, th police, or the emergency services. However, before taking this course of action, I would discus my intentions with you.

2. SESSIONS

i. We have agreed that we will meet for ten weekly sessions, each session lasting one hour. These will be on .... at .... This hour is your time, and will not be given to anyone else even if you are on holiday. Therefore, I reserve the right to charge for missed sessions. If you arrive late, I will not be able to extend your session beyond the time agreed.

ii. If for any reason I need to cancel a session, I will try to offer you an alternative appointment in the same week. However, if the time offered is not convenient for you, I will not charge fo that week's session.

3. FEES

We have agreed that you will pay £ .... per week by cheque and that if I decide to increas my fees, I will give you four weeks' notice.

4. MY HOLIDAYS

As advised, I take five weeks holiday per year, one at Christmas, one at Easter and three weeks during the summer. If it is necessary for me to take any other breaks in addition to these, I will give you as much notice as possible, and will not make any charge for sessions I cancel.

5. TERMINATION

i. If you wish to terminate counselling before the number of sessions we have contracted for, please give me at least two weeks' notice. If you fail to do this, I reserve the right to charge for all or part of my fee for the number of sessions contracted.

ii. I reserve the right to terminate counselling immediately if you commit any physical harm to me or yourself, or cause any damage to my property, counselling room, furniture, fixtures or fittings.

6. NOTES

I will make brief notes of our sessions. You cannot be identified from these notes, and they will be securely locked away. Your notes will be destroyed when our contract terminates.

7. AUDIO TAPES

Occasionally I might ask you if I can record the session to enable me to oversee my work. If I decide to do this, I will seek your permission before the session begins. You have the right to listen to any tapes made of our sessions together, and these will be erased immediately after you or I have finished with them.

8. OTHER

i. If you arrive for a session under the influence of non-prescribed drugs or alcohol, I reserve the right to cancel the session.

Please read the foregoing carefully to confirm it is what we agreed. If you are satisfied that it is correct, please sign below

Signed: .... Signed: ....
            Counsellor   Client

Fig. 7. Example of a counselling contract.

develop mutual expectations, give clients a flavor of the
mechanics of the helping process, diminish initial client
anxiety and reluctance, provide a sense of direction, and
enhance clients' freedom of choice. (1990:81)

For an example of a written counselling contract see Figure 7.

Ending the first session

It is important to end sessions on time. This helps the client
feel safe, and to understand the 'ground rules'. When a session
is nearing an end, it can be helpful to say something like: 'We
have about 10 minutes left of this session. Perhaps it would be
helpful to summarise what we have talked about today.' It can
often prove beneficial to let your client summarise what has
been discussed during the session. Something like, 'What will
you take away with you from today?' helps the client to
summarise. Your closing sentences need to be clear, and should
indicate that it's time to end the session.

Things to avoid

♦ Don't introduce **new topics** into the concluding period. If
you do this, it may confuse your client. He or she will think
that they can still go on for a while. If your client introduces
a new subject in the last few minutes of the session, you
could say: 'I can see that this is very important to you, and
I think it is an area we could look at in more depth in our
next session together. How would you feel about that?'

♦ Some clients wait until they are leaving before disclosing an
important piece of information, for example, 'Oh, by the
way...' This may reflect the client's feeling of shame or
embarrassment, or the realisation that this is their last
opportunity to 'let the cat out of the bag'. Don't be
manipulated into giving **extra time**. Again, show the client
respect by saying something like: 'I appreciate your courage
in telling me that. I can see that it wasn't easy for you, and
it sounds as if you have been holding on to that secret for a
long time. Would it help if we allocated the next session to
give the situation the attention it deserves?' Often, just

verbalising a painful secret, and being heard, can bring a tremendous sense of relief.

◆ Don't get hooked into **the presenting problem.** The problem which the client chooses to talk about, or the 'presenting problem' as it is sometimes called, is of considerable significance. It is what clients complain of, their 'admission ticket' to counselling, a 'trial balloon'. Sometimes it is something which is not of primary importance in order to test out the counsellor, but more often it represents that aspect of the client's problem which, at this present time, is giving him the most anxiety. Perhaps it would be too emotionally demanding to talk about the significant problem before the counselling relationship had been firmly established. Whatever the reasons, it is always wise to sit back and wait for the client to develop the theme. At the same time, it is essential to acknowledge the presenting problem, but being aware that there are probably other issues to be considered.

Exercise

Exercise 2

Building trust and rapport: case study

A distressed woman makes an appointment to see you. Immediately she enters the room she bursts into tears, and says: 'He has left me, and I just don't know what to do. I feel so lonely and the children are upset. What do you think I should do?'

Write a response that demonstrates that you are fully present with the client.

Example of how to build trust and rapport

'I can see you are very distraught because your partner has walked out on you, and it's hurting your children too. I'm also picking up that you feel your chances of sorting this out on your own are pretty low at the moment.'

Summary

This chapter has focused on developing the skills to help establish a safe and therapeutic environment for the client. Particular emphasis has been given to meeting, greeting and seating, boundary setting, and strategies for developing trust. The next important stage is acquiring the skills that can help clients to explore their problems.

> *When love and skill work together,*
> *Expect a masterpiece.*
>
> John Ruskin

CHAPTER 4

Helping the Client Explore the Problem

So when you are listening to somebody, completely, attentively,
then you are listening not only to the words,
but also to the feeling of what is being conveyed,
to the whole of it, not part of it.

Jiddu Krishnamurti

Having got the physical setting arranged, greeted the client, and sorted out a contract, what happens next? In this chapter we get down to the nitty gritty of effective counselling – what the counsellor does to facilitate the counselling process. We start to look more closely at some important counselling principles, qualities and skills, the first one being primary empathy. Empathy hinges on the quality of active listening. Empathy will not flourish in an atmosphere of deficient listening. The client will know we are listening by the quality of our responses and by how accurately we respond to his feelings.

To aid listening the counsellor uses a range of skills, which are developed and demonstrated through this chapter and throughout the book. Figure 8 shows the listening skills the counsellor uses to facilitate exploration of the problem.

This chapter emphasises that the skills used in counselling are those we use every day. We are not talking about extraordinary skills, although when they are tuned and refined, they can achieve extraordinary results.

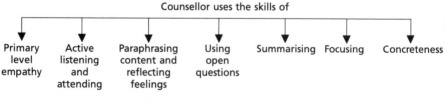

Counsellor uses the skills of

| Primary level empathy | Active listening and attending | Paraphrasing content and reflecting feelings | Using open questions | Summarising | Focusing | Concreteness |

Aim: To facilitate exploration of the problem

Fig. 8. The listening skills the counsellor uses to facilitate exploration of the problem.

Primary level empathy

Empathic responding is a vital part of active listening – hearing what the client says from the internal frame of reference, and responding in such a way that the client knows and feels that the counsellor is striving to understand. In this section we are concerned mainly with primary level empathy – that is, responding to the facts and the expressed feelings. Later on we shall work with advanced empathy, which deals with the implied facts and feelings. A helpful suggestion is to say 'You feel – because...'. The 'because' helps to tune into the content, and/or the behaviours underlying the feelings.

Examples of primary level empathy

1. Client and counsellor talking.

Client: I keep telling myself not to move too quickly with Jenny. She's so quiet, and when she does say anything, it's usually how nervous she is. It's obvious to me that when I say anything to her she gets fidgety and anxious, then I wish I hadn't opened my mouth. It's like a checkmate. If I move I push her away, and if I don't move, nothing will happen between us, and I'll lose her anyway.
(Feelings identified by counsellor: Anxious, catch-22, cautious, frustrated, protective, regret.)

Counsellor: George, you feel both protective of Jenny because you want to respect her space, yet you also feel on edge because you're afraid that the relationship is not going anywhere.

2. Two friends talking.

Daniel: I've always found you to be an easy going and a light-hearted fellow, Steve, and mostly I've enjoyed your playfulness. However, an impression that's been growing stronger for some time is that your humour is saying, 'Don't touch me'. Whenever we get into deeper things, I'm put off when you turn the discussion into a huge joke.
(Feelings identified by friend: Delight, flippant, irritated, pleasure, put off, resentment.)

Steve: You feel both pleased and irritated with the way I behave, Daniel, because I can't take anything seriously and laugh everything off, and this gets up your nose.'

Active listening

Sensitive, active listening is an important way to bring about personality changes in attitudes and the way we behave toward ourselves and others. When we listen, people tend to respond in a more emotionally mature way; become more open to experiences; become less defensive; more democratic and less authoritarian.

When we are listened to, we listen to ourselves with more care, and are able to express thoughts and feelings more clearly. Self-esteem is enhanced through active listening, because the threat of having one's ideas and feelings criticised is greatly reduced. Because we do not have to defend, we are able to see ourselves for what we truly are, and are then in a better position to change. Listening, and responding to what we hear, is influenced by our own frame of reference.

Poor listening habits identified

1. Not paying attention.
2. Pretend-listening.
3. Listening but not hearing the meaning.
4. Rehearsing what to say.
5. Interrupting the speaker in mid-sentence.
6. Hearing what is expected.
7. Feeling defensive, expecting an attack.
8. Listening for something to disagree with.

Figures 9 and 10 identify some of the blocks that can get in the way of active listening.

Knowing what to avoid

♦ When we try to get people to see themselves as we see them, or would like to see them, this is control and direction, and is more for our needs than for theirs. The less we need to evaluate, influence, control and direct, the more we enable ourselves to listen with understanding.

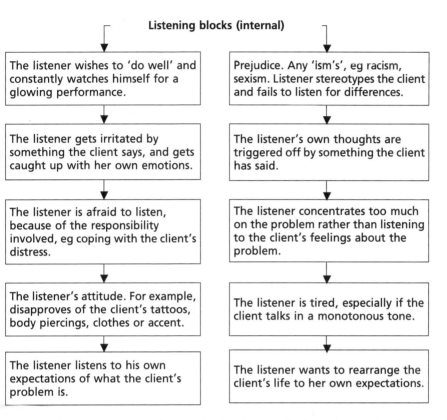

Fig. 9. Blocks that can get in the way of active listening: the listener's internal noises.

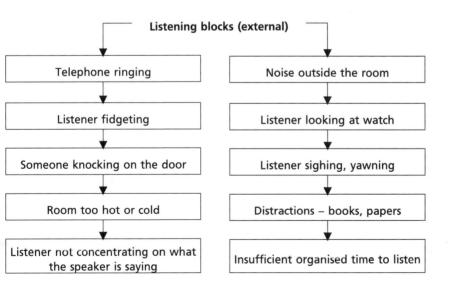

Fig. 10. Blocks that can get in the way of active listening: external noise.

♦ When we respond to the demand for decisions, actions, judgments and evaluations, or agree with someone against someone else, we are in danger of losing our objectivity. The surface question usually is the vehicle that has a deeper need as its passenger.

♦ When we shoulder responsibility for other people, we remove from them the right to be active participants in the problem-solving process. Active involvement releases energy, it does not drain it from the other person. Active participation is a process of thinking *with* people, instead of thinking *for*, or about them.

♦ Judgment – critical or favourable – is generally patronising.

♦ Platitudes and clichés demonstrate either uninterest or a verbal poverty.

♦ Verbal reassurances are insulting, for they demean the problem.

Being positive

♦ Get into the person's frame of reference.

♦ Listen for total meaning which is content and feelings. Both require hearing and responding to. In some instances the content is far less important than the feeling, for the words are but vehicles. We must try to remain sensitive to the total meaning the message has to the speaker:
   – What is she/he trying to tell me?
   – What does this mean to this person?
   – How does this person see this situation?

♦ Note all cues: not all communication is verbal. Truly sensitive listening notes:
   – body posture
   – breathing changes
   – eye movements
   – facial expression
   – hand movements
   – hesitancies
   – inflection
   – mumbled words
   – stressed words.

What we communicate by listening

We communicate interest in the importance of the speaker; respect for the speaker's thoughts, not necessarily agreement; non-evaluation; and we validate the person's worth.

Listening demonstrates, it does not tell. Listening catches on. Just as anger is normally met with anger, so listening encourages others to listen. Listening is a constructive behaviour and the person who consistently listens with understanding is the person who is most likely to be listened to.

Responding as a part of listening

Passive listening, without responding, is deadening and demeaning. We should never assume that we have really understood until we can communicate that understanding to the full satisfaction of the other person. Effective listening hinges on constant clarification to establish true understanding.

Effective listeners:

1. Put the talker at ease.
2. Limit their own talking.
3. Are attentive.
4. Remove distractions.
5. Get inside the talker's frame of reference.
6. Are patient and don't interrupt.
7. Watch for feeling words.
8. Listen to the paralinguistics.
9. Are aware of their own biases.
10. Are aware of body language.

Listening with the third ear

The phrase 'listening with the third ear' was coined by Theodor Reik, to point out the quality of psychotherapy, where active listening goes beyond the five senses. The 'third ear' hears what is said between sentences and without words, what is expressed soundlessly, what the speaker feels and thinks.

Principles for third ear listening

◆ Have a reason or purpose for listening.
◆ Suspend judgment.
◆ Resist distractions.
◆ Wait before responding.
◆ Repeat verbatim.
◆ Rephrase the message accurately.
◆ Identify important themes.
◆ Reflect content and search for meaning.
◆ Be ready to respond.

Conveying non-acceptance

We convey non-acceptance by:
◆ Advising, giving solutions – 'Why don't you   ?'
◆ Evaluating, blaming – 'You are definitely wrong...'
◆ Interpreting, analysing – 'What you need is...'
◆ Lecturing, informing – 'Here are the facts...'
◆ Name-calling, shaming – 'You are stupid...'
◆ Ordering, directing – 'You have to...'
◆ Praising, agreeing – 'You are definitely right...'
◆ Preaching, moralising – 'You ought to...'
◆ Questioning, probing – 'Why did you...?'
◆ Sympathising, supporting – 'You'll be OK...'
◆ Warning, threatening – 'You had better not...'
◆ Withdrawing, avoiding – 'Let's forget it...'

Summary

Listening is far from the passive state which some people think it is. Active listening – as it has been presented here – is a skill of great sophistication, which is available to all who would attempt to acquire and practise it. Words are vehicles for feelings, and feelings are the cement which holds together the bricks of a relationship. So it is essential to respond to both words (content) and feelings.

Responding is giving feedback, but not feedback which merely repeats what the person says – that is parroting, and deadly dull. Feedback which is careful and constructive is positive; feedback which is designed to hurt is destructive. 'Oh, you know me! A spade's a spade.' This sort of remark generally is a cover-up for lack of tact and lack of concern for other people, and has no place in effective relationships.

Attending

The greatest gift you can give another is the purity of your attention.
Richard Moss

Attending means demonstrating that we are physically and emotionally available to the client. It involves giving the client our undivided attention – listening to the facts and feelings and paying attention to the client's body language.

Attending involves:

◆ *body:* eye contact, facial expression, limbs relaxed
◆ *thoughts:* uncluttered and focused, totally engaged in listening
◆ *attitude:* open and available
◆ *feelings:* secure, calm, confident.

Attending involves full SOLER contact (an acronym coined by Gerard Egan – see Figure 11).

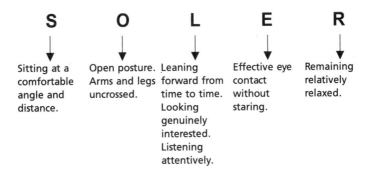

S	O	L	E	R
Sitting at a comfortable angle and distance.	Open posture. Arms and legs uncrossed.	Leaning forward from time to time. Looking genuinely interested. Listening attentively.	Effective eye contact without staring.	Remaining relatively relaxed.

Fig. 11. SOLER contact.

Minimal encouragers

Minimal encouragers demonstrate that you are attending fully to the other person. Figure 12 gives some examples.

Attending means total concentration. We can look as if we are attending, but our thoughts can be a thousand miles away. We may fool ourselves, but the other person will be intuitively aware that we have left to go on another journey. At some of the more dramatic moments of our life, just having another person with us helps us to feel in control, when otherwise we might collapse.

In relationships, ask yourself:

◆ Am I truly present and in emotional contact?
◆ Does my non-verbal behaviour reinforce my attitudes?
◆ How am I being distracted from giving my full attention?
◆ What am I doing to handle these distractions?

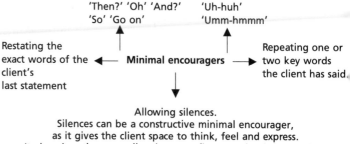

Fig. 12. Examples of minimal encouragers.

A word of caution about silences

In the early stages of counselling silences can feel very threatening to some clients and may need to be used sparingly until the therapeutic alliance is firmly established. This can be particularly true in the case of trauma survivors who:

> may have been locked in a world of silence for years, in which case talking about themselves can be an unfamiliar and daunting experience. Childhood abuse and neglect leave special scars with regard to issues of trust, and the silent counsellor may be perceived as threatening, authoritarian, all powerful, remote – even abusive. (Sutton, 1999:155)

Examples of attending responses

1. *Pat:*   'It's really embarrassing to talk about what he did.'
   Jan: 'It's embarrassing?'
   Pat: 'Yes, you see, I think it was partly my fault...'
   Jan: 'Please go on.'

2. *Paul:*   'I've tried getting another job and have sent off six application forms...'
   William: 'And?'
   Paul: 'And I've heard absolutely nothing, it's so...'
   William: 'So?'
   Paul: 'Disheartening. I almost feel like giving up.'

3. *Claire:*   'I keep cutting and burning myself.'
   Jan: 'Go on.'
   Claire: 'I feel so ashamed and disgusted with myself...'
   Jan: Leans forward towards Claire and remains silent.
   Claire: Bursts into tears and says, 'I really hate myself, and I can't take much more.'
   Jan: 'Can't take much more?'

4. *Ellen:*   'I felt so low when my Charlie died, but now...'
   William: 'But now?'
   Ellen: 'Well now I have met a kind and caring man who wants me to move in with him, but...'
   William: 'But?'
   Ellen: 'But I know my Charlie wouldn't approve – don't get me wrong – he wouldn't want me to be unhappy.'
   William: 'Tell me a bit more.'

5. *Danny:*   'I keep losing my temper – that's the problem.'
   Jan: 'Uh-huh.'
   Danny: 'It's got me into trouble – I nearly got sent to prison.'
   Jan: 'Sent to prison.'

Paraphrasing

Paraphrasing means restating the thoughts and feelings of the client's words in your own. Paraphrasing can bring clarification. It means reflecting the content, mirroring the literal meaning of the communication (see Figure 13).

Sometimes paraphrasing is necessary; at other times reflecting feelings is more appropriate. In every communication, words are vehicles for feelings, so it is essential to hear and respond to both content and feeling.

When listening, we focus initially upon the content. In doing so, we want to be sure that we have all the details of the client's experiences. Otherwise we will not be able to help the client to understand them.

> *A paraphrased response will capture the main points communicated.*

Focusing on content

WHO? WHAT? WHY? WHEN? WHERE? HOW?
I keep six honest serving-men
(They taught me all I knew);
Their names are What and Why and When
And How and Where and Who.

Just So Stories 'The Elephant's Child', Rudyard Kipling (1902)

If we can supply answers to these questions, we can be sure that we have the basic ingredients of the other person's experience.

Useful formats for responding to content are:
- 'You're saying _____'
  or
- 'In other words _____'
  or
- 'It sounds as if _____'

However, if we're not careful, such responses can sound stilted and stereotyped. Try to retain freshness.

Paraphrasing is not parroting

A paraphrase is a brief response in the hearer's own words that captures the main points of the content of what the other person has said. It may condense or expand what has been said. In general conversation many assumptions are made about what has been said. Counselling is not an 'ordinary' conversation.

> *Effective paraphrasing is part of effective listening which ensures understanding.*

Words carry feelings, so not only is it necessary to understand the client's words, we must also try to understand why particular words, in preference to others, are used.

If clients have been expressing their thoughts with difficulty then this is a good time to paraphrase. Letting clients hear the meaning as understood by someone else may help them to clarify more precisely what they do mean. Paraphrasing may echo feeling words without responding to them.

Examples of paraphrasing

Andrew, your friend, says to you in an emotionally flat voice, and delivered with short pauses between words and sentences:

> I used to ... enjoy going out and having ... fun. Now I have to really force myself, and I, I ... don't enjoy myself any more. All the time I just have a, a ... feeling of (longer pause) sadness. I'm not really part of the group any more.

The key words and phrases here are: going out, fun, force, sadness, not part of.

Response

In the past, Andrew, you had a great time socialising. Right now, however, you've lost your drive, and don't get much pleasure from going out and meeting people. For a lot of the time you feel down and flat and not really part of what's going on around you.

Susan, a student colleague, says to you, over coffee:

I don't expect Sam to help with *all* the household chores, but he knows very well I need time to study for my nursing finals. I can't spend all my spare time cooking and cleaning and waiting on him hand and foot.

The key words and phrases here are: expect, chores, time, exams, hand and foot.

Response

Susan, you would like Sam to support you more, and take his share of the work around the house, so that you can find more time to study instead of running after him. You would like a bit more sharing.

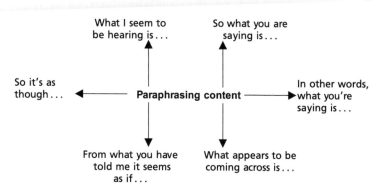

Fig. 13. Examples of paraphrasing content.

To conclude this section on paraphrasing content we continue our dialogue with the five clients referred to in attending responses (see page 43).

1. *Pat*   'So what you are saying is you think you are partly responsible in some way.'

2. *Paul*   'It sounds as if not getting any replies to your applications for work is making your wonder whether it's worth bothering any more.'

3. *Claire*   'From what you have told me it seems as though you are having a difficult time right now, and you wonder how much more you can take.'

4. *Ellen*   'What you seem to be saying is that you feel you would be letting Charlie down in some way if you accepted this man's offer.'

5. *Danny*   'What seems to be coming across is that your anger is getting you into real trouble, and the magistrates have recommended you learn some techniques for handling it more constructively.'

Reflecting feelings

Reflecting concentrates on the feelings within a statement. Paraphrasing and reflecting are invariably linked. In practice, it may be artificial to try to separate them. Reflecting feelings accurately depends on empathic understanding.

In listening to someone who is talking about a problem, neither pity nor sympathy is constructive because both are highly subjective. Reflecting involves both listening and understanding and communicating that understanding. If our understanding remains locked up within us, we contribute little to the communication.

Being able to reflect feelings involves viewing the world from the other person's frame of reference, thoughts, feelings and behaviours. Effective responding indicates a basic acceptance of people.

Reflecting does not act as a communication 'stopper' on the flow of talk, on emotions, or make people feel inadequate, inferior, defensive, or as though they are being patronised. Effective responses are made in language that is easily understood. They have a clarity and freshness of expression. Effective responses are accompanied by good vocal and bodily communication. Figure 14 gives examples of responses.

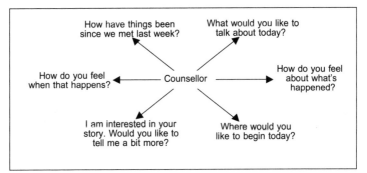

Fig. 14. Some open questions.

Responding effectively

Choosing the right time to respond is important. To respond effectively:

◆ Observe facial and bodily movements.
◆ Listen to the words and their meanings.
◆ Tune into your own emotional reactions to what the client is communicating.
◆ Sense the meaning of the communication.
◆ Take into account the degree of the client's self-awareness.
◆ Respond appropriately and so facilitate communication.
◆ Use vocal and bodily language that are congruent with each other.
◆ Check out the accuracy of your understanding.
◆ Use real, rather than stereotyped, language.

Examples of stereotyped responses:

◆ 'Thank you for sharing.'
◆ 'Am I on the right track?'
◆ 'Am I getting the picture?'
◆ 'Have a good day.'

Such phrases frequently pepper counselling literature, so much that the word sharing has lost much of its meaning.

◆ 'You have shared many deep feelings today' would be appropriate.

Examples of reflecting feelings

Alex says:

I'm 23, but I'll have to leave home soon. I'm not sure I'll cope though. Mum and Dad smother me, and can't see why I want to lead my own life.

The key words are: have to cope, smother, own life.

Counsellor:

Alex, you sound confused and very uncertain that you would be doing the right thing, moving away from home. You feel suffocated by your parents, and want your independence, but it seems as if the price of this is having to separate from your parents.

Christine says:

> I'd just had enough of Dave. You should have heard the way he yelled at Emma. I mean, she's only ten months old. Did I do the right thing? Should we try again?

The key words are: enough, she's only, should we.

Counsellor:

> Christine, what I hear is that you have regrets about leaving Dave and you are wondering whether you should attempt a reconciliation. At the same time you are concerned for Emma's safety. You would like me to tell you what to do to resolve this conflict.

To conclude this section we use reflecting feelings responses with the five clients Pat, Paul, Claire, Ellen and Danny.

Counsellor reflecting feelings responses:

1. *Pat*   'You feel ashamed about what happened because you feel you were partly to blame.'

2. *Paul*   'I can see that you feel despondent and disappointed because you have put a lot of effort into applying for jobs and nobody has offered you an interview.'

3. *Claire*   'So you feel as if you are at the end of your tether, and I'm also picking up that you feel embarrassed and perhaps loathe yourself because you can't stop hurting yourself.'

4. *Ellen*   'I can see that you feel confused because you have met a nice man who wants you to move in with him. You know that Charlie would want you to be happy, but you feel he would not approve of you living with another man.'

5. *Danny*   'You feel resentful because the magistrates have told you to come, and that you have no choice in the matter.'

Asking the right questions

Basically, there are two types of questions: open questions which help the flow of communication and encourage the speaker to elaborate or be more specific, and closed questions which tend to shut communication down. Closed questions are those that can be answered with a 'Yes' or 'No'. For example: 'Did you...' 'Do you think that...?', 'Are you going to...?' They are useful for seeking factual information (Sutton, 2000: 127).

Some common pitfalls in asking questions

1. Asking two or more questions at the same time, which create confusion in the client's mind. Usually the client wi answer the last question asked.
2. Wrongly timed questions that interrupt and hinder the helping process.
3. Asking too many questions which may give the impression that we can provide solutions to other people's problems.
4. Asking too many questions, which may give the impression of an interrogation.

The emphasis in counselling is on using questions to help people solve their own problems.

Open questions

Asking open questions encourages the client to express their thoughts and feelings (see Figure 15). Open questions:

♦ seek clarification
♦ encourage exploration
♦ establish mutual understanding
♦ gauge feelings.

Open questions normally start with:

♦ **What** – for example: 'What happened then?'
♦ **How** – for example: 'How do you feel about your parents splitting up?'
♦ **When** – for example: 'When would you like to make the break?'

though that is not all there is to creating open questions.
When we accompany a statement with:

♦ Could it be?
♦ Do you think/feel?
♦ Does this mean?

- Have you considered?
- Am I (would I be) right?
- Is that...?
- Don't you think?

it usually means a closed question.

Things to avoid

1. **Closed questions** – unless you want to elicit information or establish facts. 'How old are you?' or 'Do you like your mother?' or 'Do you think counselling is helping you?' are examples of closed questions.

2. **Prying questions** – which are asked out of your curiosity about areas not yet opened up by the client. 'Tell me about your sex life', when sex has not been mentioned.

3. **Limiting questions** – such as, 'Don't you think that...?' 'Isn't it a fact that ...'

4. **Punishing questions** – the purpose of which is to expose the other person without appearing to, and puts the person on the spot: 'With your vast experience you can answer the question, surely?'

5. **Hypothetical questions** – which are often motivated by criticism: 'If you were making that report, wouldn't you say it differently?' Such questions typically begin with 'If', 'What if', 'How about'.

6. **Demand or command questions** – which are designed to impress urgency or importance. 'Have you done anything about...?'

7. **Screened questions** – which are designed to get the other person to make a decision that fits with your hidden wish. This type of question puts great pressure on the person being questioned who is not sure what answer is required: 'Would you like to go to...?'

8. **Leading questions** – which manoeuvre the other person into a vulnerable position. Leading questions are often used in court to confuse the witness. 'Is it fair to say that you...?' 'Would you agree that...?'

9. **Rhetorical questions** – which forestall a response because the questioner fears it may not be a favourable one. Such questions attempt to secure a guaranteed agreement. No response is required: 'I'm coming for the weekend, OK?'

10. **'Now I've got you' questions** – where the motive is to dig a trap for the other person to fall into: 'Weren't you the one who...?'

11. **Statements that sound like questions** – 'You argue with your partner a lot, don't you?'

* Asking appropriate questions can assist in clarifying something that is not quite clear. 'I don't understand. Do you mean . . .?' will usually help the client by letting her see that the counsellor is still with her.

Questions normally should be based on material already provided by the client, rather than based on the counsellor's curiosity. Facts may be necessary, but not to the extent that they impede the client from talking.

Questions should never intrude into the counselling process. They should always be a natural part of what is going on, and the client should always be able to understand the relevance of the question at the time it is asked. There is a time to ask a question and a time not to.

* From *Counselling in Nursing*, Stewart W. (1983) Harper & Row

Useful aids:

◆ Respond to what the person has said, rather than asking questions.

Think of the counselling process as building a wall, brick by brick. The client makes a statement (brick one), followed by the counsellor's statement (brick two), and so on. In this way, we do not rush ahead and cause anxiety by pushing indelicately into sensitive areas not yet ready to be explored.

To conclude this section we use open questions with the five clients Pat, Paul, Claire, Ellen and Danny.

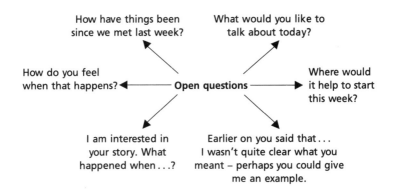

Fig. 15. Examples of open questions.

Counsellor using an open question:

1. *Pat*   'Can we take a look at what makes you feel you are partly responsible for what happened?'

2. *Paul*   'Can you tell me what sort of jobs you have been applying for?'

3. *Claire* 'Can you describe the feelings you get that make you want to harm yourself?'

4. *Ellen*   'Perhaps you would like to tell me how you feel about moving in with this man – what's his name?'

5. *Danny*   'When you got angry and ended up in trouble, what did you do exactly?'

Summarising

Summarising is the process of tying together all that has been talked about during part or all of the counselling session. It attempts to draw together the main threads of what has been discussed. It clarifies what has been accomplished and what still needs to be done.

Summarising enables the counsellor to get a better understanding of the client's view of things, and enables the client to see what progress has been made. When summarising, the counsellor should pull together the most relevant points, state them as simply and clearly as possible, and then check with the client the accuracy of the summary.

Summarising should not be overdone and should not be experienced by the client as an intrusion. Summarising may happen at any time during a session – it can be particularly valuable to highlight recurring themes. A summary at the end of a session is vital for several reasons. It gives the client an opportunity to hear again the main points; it gives the counsellor an opportunity to clarify and consolidate her understanding of what has taken place; it provides an opportunity for both, and particularly the client, to think about the next session. (Paraphrased from Stewart, 1983.)

The aim of summarising

 ◆ To outline relevant facts, thoughts, feelings and meanings.
 ◆ To prompt further exploration of a particular theme.
 ◆ To close the discussion on a particular theme.
 ◆ To help both counsellor and client find direction.
 ◆ To move the interview forward.

Summarising may:
 ◆ include a mixture of what was said and what was implied
 ◆ focus scattered facts, thoughts, feelings and meanings.

Summarising should:
 ◆ be simple, clear and jargon-free
 ◆ be checked for accuracy
 ◆ catch the essential meanings.

Figure 16 gives examples of summarising responses.

Case studies

Rachel, age 20

Rachel went to an office party and was driven home by one of her male colleagues. She invited him in for coffee. He started kissing her, and when she protested, he began touching her intimately. Rachel tried to fight him off, but he ended up raping her.

She says:

I can't believe what happened. I mean there was no 'come on' from me. Just being friendly, and that's what he did. Like a wild animal. He was too strong. I was screaming, he just laughed. How can I face him now? What should I do? If only I hadn't gone to that party.

Counsellor: (Sits in silence until Rachel stops sobbing.)

Rachel, I can see how distressed you are *(empathic responding)*. You're bewildered that an innocent invitation could turn into such a traumatic and terrifying experience like rape. Your efforts to fight him off were useless; he was like someone demented. You wish you hadn't gone to the party, and you're not sure how you can face him. You are hoping I will tell you what to do.

Jane, 20
Jane says:

I have strong religious beliefs that sex outside marriage is wrong. Alan has tried to persuade me to have sex because he would like me to have a baby. He has told me if I have a baby, he will be sure that I am truly in love with him. But the whole idea of having a baby outside marriage is too much for me. Alan says he is not ready for marriage and settling down yet, and I would like to carry on with my career in teaching. If I do what he wants I'm not being true to myself, and if I don't I'll probably lose him.

Counsellor:

Jane, you seem very confused with all that's happening in your life right now (*empathic responding*). Your boyfriend wants you to have a baby, but you're not sure about that. It's important for you to be married before you consider having a family, but Alan doesn't think the same way. For the moment you would like to continue with your teaching career because that is important to you. You are afraid if you stick to your principles, Alan might end your relationship.

Examples of summarising responses

To conclude this section we use summarising responses with Pat, Paul, Claire, Ellen and Danny.

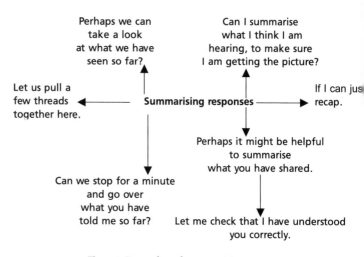

Fig. 16. Examples of summarising responses.

Pat

Pat responds to an open question with:

> Well, we both had too much to drink and he offered to take me home. I asked him in for coffee and then he...he...raped me.

Counsellor responds with:

> Can I check out that I am understanding you correctly? Thanks. What I hear you saying is that both of you were worse the wear from alcohol, and when he took you home you invited him in for coffee, and it ended up with you being raped. You feel you are to blame in some way because you let him into your home.

Paul

Paul responds to an open question with:

> Well, I've applied for three posts as manager for different engineering companies, and three for the position of supervisor with manufacturing plants. I don't have much experience in anything else.

Counsellor responds with:

> Can we recap on what you have told me so far? You have applied to three engineering firms for the post of manager

and to three manufacturing plants for the post of supervisor. You feel your experience in other fields is a bit limited, and this may be holding you back?

Claire

Claire responds to an open question with:

> I get these terrible feelings of panic and anger, and get very distressed. The only way I can stop them is to cut myself. It's the only thing that makes the pain go away.

Counsellor responds with:

> Claire, can I summarise what you have said to ensure that I am understanding you correctly? Thank you. Before you cut yourself you experience overwhelming feelings of anxiety and rage which are very upsetting for you. These dreadful and frightening feelings just won't leave you, and cutting yourself is the only thing that gives you any relief.

Ellen

Ellen responds to an open question with:

> His name is Peter, and in many ways I would like to move in with him. I enjoy his company and he has a great sense of humour – he really makes me laugh. He's ever so kind too; nothing is too much trouble, and he says he loves me a lot. But, I can't stop thinking what my Charlie would think of me – I'm sure he wouldn't like me living with another man.

Counsellor responds with:

> Ellen, could I tell you what I think I am hearing, to see if I am understanding you correctly? A big part of you would like to share your life with Peter because you have a lot of fun and laughs together. He loves you and is very thoughtful and caring. However, you have convinced yourself that Charlie would disapprove, which is leaving you in a dilemma.

Danny

Danny responds to an open question with:

Well, there was a fight at the club, and I threw a chair at someone. It hit him on the head and he had to go to hospital and get it stitched. The police arrived and I hurled a bit of verbal at them, so they arrested me and threw me in a cell, telling me to calm down and sleep it off. Next morning I was up before the magistrates charged with A.B.H. (actual bodily harm).

Counsellor responds with:

Danny, can we stop for a minute to go over what you have told me so far. You got involved in a brawl, lost your temper and injured someone. You were verbally abusive towards the police so they arrested you and held you overnight. You found yourself in court next morning on a charge of actual bodily harm.

Focusing

Focusing implies a certain degree of counsellor direction and guidance of the exploration. Clients often need help to get to grips with complex problems. Everything cannot be worked out at once. Focusing uses specific questions to tease out detail and to explore particular topics in depth. (See Figure 17 for examples of focusing responses.) Focusing helps client and counsellor to find out where to start, and in which direction to continue.

Principles to bear in mind

If there is a crisis, first help the client to manage the crisis. Focus on issues that the client sees as important. Begin with a problem that seems to be causing the client pain. Begin with some manageable part of the problem.

Examples

1. Carol, in her mid 30s, was left a widow 18 months ago. She is experiencing financial difficulties. A male friend has suggested she lives with him but this means moving some distance away and her children do not want to move.

All of these issues are important and some of them will take longer than others to resolve. Helping Carol get her finances sorted out would be the most practical, and release energy to deal with some of the other issues.

Response

> I've heard what you've been saying, and there is a lot there. It seems as if the main strands are... Which do you think is the most urgent issue to explore first?

2. George, aged 80, is dying of cancer. As the pastoral counsellor, Anne, listens to him, she picks up George's concern for his wife. At the same time, she detects underlying fears about his own death, fear he is not admitting to.

Anne's response

> George, I hear a number of issues you would probably like to talk about, not necessarily right now. My hunch is that the one you would like to spend time talking over is your concern for your wife, and how she is managing.

Types of response

The 'contrast response'

The term 'contrast response' describes a marked awareness of the differences between two conditions or events which results from bringing them together: 'If you think about staying in your present job, or moving to another job, what would it be like then?'

Example

> The counsellor says: 'Carol, perhaps we can take a look at what we have seen so far. Your husband died 18 months ago, and since then you have had financial worries. Fred has asked you to go and live with him. However, this means moving away from the area, and your children are very reluctant to go. If you think about your life as it is now, and then think about Fred's offer to live with him, what differences do you think it will make?'

The 'choice-point response'

The term 'choice-point' describes any set of circumstances in which a choice among several alternatives is required: 'From what you've said, it looks as if these are the major issues (itemising them). Which of these would you feel most comfortable working with first?'

Example

> The counsellor says: 'Carol, let's pull a few things together here. Sadly, your husband died 18 months ago, and you are left with the children to cope with on your own. Fred has asked you to move in with him, but your children are opposed to the idea of moving away. You are also very concerned about how you are managing financially. It seems as if there are a lot of separate issues we could talk about, and I'm wondering which one you would like to focus on first?'

The 'figure-ground response'

The term 'figure-ground' describes how a person perceives the relationship between the object of the attention or focus, the figure, and the rest of what is around, the perceptual field, the ground. The figure generally has form or structure and appears to be in front of the ground. The figure is given shape or form and the background is left unshaped and lacking in form. 'These are the various points of the problem, it seems to me that the most worthwhile to address first could be the need for you to get a job. How do you feel about that?'

Thus, figure-ground focusing helps to give one part of the problem shape and form and so helps the client to more readily grasp hold of something and work with it.

Example

> The counsellor says: 'Carol, can we stop for a minute and look at what you have told me so far? First, there's the issue of managing your finances. Second, there's the issue of whether you should live with Fred. Third, there's the issue of your children not wanting to move away from the area. noticed when you mentioned your financial situation that

you looked extremely anxious, and my feeling is that
working on the finances might be beneficial to begin with.
How does that sound to you?'

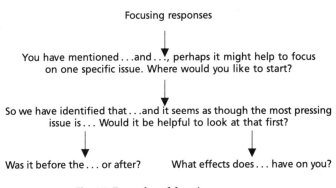

Fig. 17. Examples of focusing responses.

Examples of focusing responses

Let's pick up again with the five clients, Pat, Paul, Claire, Ellen
and Danny, and see how the counsellor might use focusing
responses.

Pat

Counsellor responds to Pat with:

You have told me you were raped by this man, and that
you feel you may have brought it on yourself in some way.
There appear to be two issues here, and it seems as if being
raped is causing you a great deal of distress. How do you
feel about exploring that first? (*figure-ground*).

Paul

Counsellor responds to Paul with:

You mentioned that you have applied for six different jobs
without success, and you feel your lack of experience in
areas other than engineering and manufacturing might be a
stumbling block. Perhaps it might be helpful to focus on
one specific issue. What would be most helpful for you to
talk about first? (*choice-point*).

Claire

Counsellor responds to Claire with:

You have shared with me some of the feelings you get before you harm yourself. You have also told me that these feelings won't go away, and that you feel compelled to cut and burn yourself as a way of escaping from these awful feelings. When you spoke about cutting yourself I noticed you rubbing the scar on your wrist, which looks very painful and raw. I wonder whether it would help to talk about that scar and what it means to you? (*figure-ground*).

Ellen

Counsellor responds to Ellen with:

You say that a big part of you wants to share your life with Peter, but you feel Charlie would disapprove, and this leaves you feeling that you would be disloyal to Charlie in some way. There seems to be a lot of painful issues we could talk about, Ellen, and I'm wondering which one it would be most helpful for you to talk about first? (*choice-point*).

Danny

Counsellor responds to Danny with:

Danny, from where I am sitting there seems to be a lot of issues involved here. First, there's the issue of your anger and aggression which you seem to have difficulty controlling. Second, there's the issue of your drinking which seems to spark your anger and aggression. Third, there's the issue of injuring someone as a result of not being able to control your anger, and fourth there's the issue of having a criminal record and how this might affect your life in the future. If you could look ahead a bit, how different would you like things to look for you in the future? (*contrast*).

Being concrete to help the client be more specific

Being concrete means being able to get clients to be concrete or specific, although at times it can be quite difficult, yet it is essential if they are to come to terms fully with whatever is causing them concern. The opposite of being concrete, direct and specific is making 'generalised' (indirect and vague) statements. So often in general conversation as well as in counselling we confuse the issue by not being concrete, specific and direct. A generalisation does not discriminate but lumps all parts together.

A generality that is common in everyday speech is 'you'. Clients who say, 'You never know when people approve of what you're doing', when encouraged to rephrase it to, 'I never know when people approve of what I'm doing', will usually be able to perceive their statement in a different light. The client needs to be able to identify thoughts, feelings, behaviour and experiences in specific ways. Personalising a statement in this way makes it pertinent and real. In one sense it is owning the problem. Being specific opens the way for a realistic acknowledgement of feelings.

Overcoming client resistance

Owning, and not merely reporting, such feelings opens the door to exploring them. While this may be uncomfortable for the client, it is vital. Sometimes thoughts, feelings and behaviours are expressed before the counselling relationship has been established firmly enough to explore them. If such thoughts, feelings and behaviours are central to the client's problem the client will return to them at some stage. Concreteness requires clients to be prepared to examine themselves closely, and not to hide behind the facade of generality.

Clients may fiercely resist attempts to encourage them to be specific, particularly about feelings. They may have to be led gently into what, for many, is a new experience. Counsellors can collude with clients by allowing them to talk about feelings second-hand, as if they belonged to other people and not to them. 'Is this how *you* feel?' or 'Is that something like *your* situation?' (even though both of these are closed questions) may be enough to bring the interview back into focus from second-hand reporting, to 'This is what is happening to me, *now.*'

Questions to aid concreteness

Elaboration questions give the client the opportunity to expand on what has already been talked about. For example:

◆ 'Would you care to elaborate?'
◆ 'What else is there?'
◆ 'Could you expand on what you've just said?'
◆ 'Is there anything else you wish to say about . . . ?'

Specification questions aim to elicit detail about a problem. For example:

◆ 'When you say he upsets you, what precisely happens?'
◆ 'When?'
◆ 'You mentioned that . . . can you give me a specific example?'
◆ 'How many times?'

Focusing on feelings questions aim to elicit the feelings generated by a problem area. For example:

◆ 'How do you feel about that?'
◆ 'Would you care to describe your feelings?'
◆ 'Is it possible that you are feeling. . .?'

Personal responsibility questions imply not only that the other has a responsibility for owning the problem, but also for making the choices that contribute to solving it. For example:

◆ 'Are there any other things you can think of that might help you to achieve your goal?'
◆ 'How do you see your part in the break up?'
◆ 'What skills do you need to develop to solve the problem?'
◆ 'In what ways could you improve the situation?'

Examples

Mavis, to Marion, the works supervisor

Mavis (*generalised and vague*) 'I know I haven't been very regular at work recently, I haven't been very well. That's the truth of it.'

Mavis (*concrete and specific*): 'I know that over the past month I've been off work six times. I've been attending the doctor for about six months with vague abdominal pains. They haven't ye reached a firm diagnosis, but they think it's probably something to do with the gall bladder.'

Robert, to Joy, the school counsellor

Robert (*generalised and vague*): 'People keep picking on me.'
Robert (*concrete and specific*): 'My classmates pick on me because I wear glasses.'

Trudy, student teacher, to Liz, her supervisor

Trudy (*generalised and vague*): 'I know I'm dreadfully inconsistent in my work.'
Trudy (*concrete and specific*): 'I make all sorts of teaching plans, yet when it comes to the day, I don't stick to them. I think the students run the class, not me.'

Examples of encouraging questions

Let us resume once again with the five clients, Pat, Paul, Claire, Ellen and Danny, and see examples of questions the counsellor might use to encourage them to be more concrete or specific.

Pat
Counsellor to Pat: 'You say you feel you may have brought the rape on yourself in some way. To help me understand, can you be a bit more specific?' (*specification question*).

Paul
Counsellor to Paul: 'You say that have applied for six different jobs and haven't had any replies. How does this make you feel?' (*focusing on feelings question*).

Claire
Counsellor to Claire: 'Can you talk me through what thoughts are going through your mind just before you cut yourself?' (*elaboration question*).

Ellen
Counsellor to Ellen: 'You have told me that a large part of you wants to share your life with Peter. Can you tell me specifically

what appeals to you about moving in with him?'

Danny

Counsellor to Danny: 'Danny, you say that you injured another man, and this happened after you had a lot to drink. How much do you think your drinking contributed towards you becoming angry and aggressive?' (*personal responsibility question*).

Summary

To help the client explore the problem the counsellor uses the skills of:

- primary level empathy
- active listening
- attending
- paraphrasing content
- reflecting feelings
- using open questions
- summarising
- focusing
- concreteness.

Exercises

Suggested framework on how to formulate responses for the case study exercises.

1. Read every sentence in the case study carefully.

2. Identify the **facts**.

3. Identify the **expressed** feelings.

4. Identify the **implied** feelings, those that lie beneath the surface, those that are being hinted at, those that strike a chord within you.

5. Think of as many words as possible to describe the feelings.

6. Put the whole lot together in one response.

Exercise 3

Primary level empathy – case study 1 – Julie

Julie says: 'It's difficult here tonight, I can't seem to get involved with the group. We've been going an hour, and everything has been so painful. I'm not up to it right now. I get the impression that all my friends' relationships are parting at the seams, and when that happens here in the group too (pause) well, I'd like to be understanding and accepting, and all that, but I'd rather run away right now.'

Identify the feelings, then outline a response of about four to six lines.

Primary level empathy – case study 2 – Margaret to Keith

'Keith, you're usually warm and accepting with me, but I'm still not sure of where I stand with you. I guess I want you to be affectionate with me, and that's not you. Maybe what I'm saying is that I need a lot of attention. I know that whenever I say something, I expect you to understand how I'm feeling. I'm wondering now if I've been putting too many demands on you?'

Identify the feelings, then outline a response of about four to six lines.

Primary level empathy – case study 3 – Matthew

Matthew says, 'Six months ago, I wouldn't have dreamed I'd be saying what I'm about to say, to one person, maybe, but not to a group of people. That says a lot for what I feel about this group. I want you to know, I'm gay. Knowing that about me may help you understand the way I react. But more than that, I'm uneasy about my sexuality. It bothers me and makes me uncertain about who I am. That's the uncertain chap you see here. I think I can say this now because I trust you to understand me and not to think of me as a problem person who needs help.'

Identify the feelings, then outline a response of about four to six lines.

This is the end of the primary level empathy exercises. Turn to Appendix 2 for suggested responses.

Exercise 4

Listening

Read each statement carefully and assess whether the client feels listened to or not. Tick the box you think is correct.

		Listened to	Not listened to
1.	You cut me off and start telling me about your experiences.	☐	☐
2.	You accept me as I am – warts and all.	☐	☐
3.	You don't hide behind barriers.	☐	☐
4.	You want to solve my problem for me.	☐	☐
5.	You try to grasp my meaning when I feel confused.	☐	☐
6.	You resist the temptation to give me good advice.	☐	☐
7.	You hand me back the compliment I have given you.	☐	☐
8.	You resist from telling me that funny joke you are dying to tell me.	☐	☐
9.	You get embarrassed and avoid what I want to say.	☐	☐
10.	You need to feel successful.	☐	☐
11.	You allow me to express my negative feelings towards you without becoming defensive.	☐	☐
12.	You give me your undivided attention.		
13.	You make judgments about me because of my language, grammar or accent.	☐	☐
14.	You do not judge my beliefs even when they conflict with yours.	☐	☐
15.	You gaze out of the window.	☐	☐
16.	You trust me to find my own solution to my problem.	☐	☐
17.	You plan my action for me, instead of letting me find my own action.	☐	☐
18.	You allow me time to think, feel and express.	☐	☐
19.	You tap your fingers on the arm of the chair.	☐	☐
20.	You speak with enthusiasm and at an appropriate volume.	☐	☐

21. You choose an appropriate time to respond. ☐   ☐
22. You do not look at me when I am speaking. ☐   ☐
23. You enable me to make my experience feel important.   ☐   ☐
24. You keep fidgeting.   ☐   ☐
25. You keep looking at your watch.   ☐   ☐
26. You look down your nose at me.   ☐   ☐
27. You say you understand before you have heard what I have to say.   ☐   ☐
28. You have a solution to my problem before I have had the opportunity to explore my problem fully.   ☐   ☐
29. You interrupt me before I have finished talking.   ☐   ☐
30. You are not aware of the feelings behind my words.   ☐   ☐
31. You look directly at me, and face me.   ☐   ☐
32. You use open and appropriate gestures.   ☐   ☐
33. You quietly enter my internal world and try to grasp how it feels to be me.   ☐   ☐
34. You allow me to express myself even if you don't agree with my language.   ☐   ☐
35. You accept my gift of thanks.   ☐   ☐
36. You don't preach morals or condemn me for my behaviour.   ☐   ☐
37. You are interested in everything I have to say. ☐   ☐
38. You spend an hour with me and make that time feel very special.   ☐   ☐
39. You do not laugh at me, or ridicule me.   ☐   ☐
40. You are kind, gentle and encouraging.   ☐   ☐
41. You try to understand me because you really care.   ☐   ☐
42. You try to help me become liberated from the destructive barriers I have erected with sensitivity and gentleness.   ☐   ☐
43. You lean towards me and tilt your head.   ☐   ☐
44. You cross your legs and fold your arms.   ☐   ☐
45. You talk at me instead of talking with me.   ☐   ☐

This is the end of the listening exercise. Turn to Appendix 2 for the answers.

Summary

The eight blocks which affect active listening:
1. lack of trust
2. misinterpreting what is said
3. using stereotyped language
4. the words themselves
5. emotions and feelings
6. intellectualising
7. conceptualising
8. cultural.

Exercise 5

Paraphrasing – case study 1 – Alex

Alex says, 'I'm 23, but I'll have to leave home. I'm not sure how I'll cope though. Mum and Dad smother me, and can't see why I want to lead my own life.'

Outline a paraphrase. First of all identify the key words or phrases, then write down your response.

Paraphrasing – case study 2 – James

James says, 'I want to take up nursing but my mates are giving me a hard time, they say it's only a job for women and gays, not real men. It's the job for me though. What should I do?'

Outline a paraphrase. First of all identify the key words or phrases, then write down your response.

This is the end of the paraphrasing exercises. Turn to Appendix 2 for suggested responses.

Exercise 6

Reflecting feelings

To enable us to reflect feelings it helps to develop a wide vocabulary of feeling words.

List up to four different words or phrases for the statements given below.

I feel abandoned	*You feel*	_____ _____ _____ _____
I feel afraid	*You feel*	_____ _____ _____ _____
I feel aimless	*You feel*	_____ _____ _____ _____
I feel angry	*You feel*	_____ _____ _____ _____
I feel anguished	*You feel*	_____ _____ _____ _____
I feel antagonistic	*You feel*	_____ _____ _____ _____
I feel anxious	*You feel*	_____ _____ _____ _____
I feel appreciated	*You feel*	_____ _____ _____ _____
I feel apprehensive	*You feel*	_____ _____ _____ _____
I feel ashamed	*You feel*	_____ _____ _____ _____
I feel bitter	*You feel*	_____ _____ _____ _____
I feel bored	*You feel*	_____ _____ _____ _____
I feel confused	*You feel*	_____ _____ _____ _____
I feel delighted	*You feel*	_____ _____ _____ _____
I feel depressed	*You feel*	_____ _____ _____ _____
I feel devastated	*You feel*	_____ _____ _____ _____
I feel doubtful	*You feel*	_____ _____ _____ _____
I feel energetic	*You feel*	_____ _____ _____ _____
I feel envious	*You feel*	_____ _____ _____ _____
I feel embarrassed	*You feel*	_____ _____ _____ _____
I feel empty	*You feel*	_____ _____ _____ _____
I feel exasperated	*You feel*	_____ _____ _____ _____
I feel excited	*You feel*	_____ _____ _____ _____
I feel grief	*You feel*	_____ _____ _____ _____
I feel guilty	*You feel*	_____ _____ _____ _____
I feel helpless	*You feel*	_____ _____ _____ _____
I feel hopeless	*You feel*	_____ _____ _____ _____
I feel hurt	*You feel*	_____ _____ _____ _____

I feel inadequate	*You feel*	___ ___ ___ ___
I feel inferior	*You feel*	___ ___ ___ ___
I feel lonely	*You feel*	___ ___ ___ ___
I feel lost	*You feel*	___ ___ ___ ___
I feel miserable	*You feel*	___ ___ ___ ___
I feel numb	*You feel*	___ ___ ___ ___
I feel overwhelmed	*You feel*	___ ___ ___ ___
I feel rejected	*You feel*	___ ___ ___ ___
I feel sad	*You feel*	___ ___ ___ ___
I feel shocked	*You feel*	___ ___ ___ ___
I feel silly	*You feel*	___ ___ ___ ___
I feel stifled	*You feel*	___ ___ ___ ___
I feel tense	*You feel*	___ ___ ___ ___
I feel tired	*You feel*	___ ___ ___ ___
I feel trapped	*You feel*	___ ___ ___ ___
I feel useless	*You feel*	___ ___ ___ ___
I feel vulnerable	*You feel*	___ ___ ___ ___

When you have finished, turn to Appendix 2 and compare your answers.

Exercise 7

Reflecting feelings – case study 1 – Mary

Mary says, 'I will be a success. I can do it if I work hard. If it takes 18 hours a day chained to a VDU, I'll do it. If husband and family suffer, too bad. I hope they don't, but it'll be worth it in the end. Success is what matters to me.'

Identify the key words, then create a response of about six lines.

Reflecting feelings – case study 2 - Sam

Sam says, 'I can never find the time to do the things I enjoy. I'm just getting ready to go out for a swim, or go jogging, when Bill reminds me there's some letters to write to customers, or Susan collars me into helping with some household chores. It's getting increasingly difficult to get the fun out of life that I expect to have. It's depressing.'

Identify the key words, then create a response of about six lines.

This is the end of the reflecting feelings exercises. Turn to Appendix 2 for suggested responses.

Exercise 8

Open questions – case study 1 - Joe

Joe says, 'Honestly, I don't know what to do. It sounds really silly, I'm 28 but I'm afraid of women. I like them, I think, but I never know what to do. Maybe it's because I like them too much. I start to get to know a girl, and it's OK. Then I just fall head over heels for her. It scares me. I always end up getting hurt. That's how it's happened before, and that's how it is with Emma.'

Here are five closed questions:

1. How many times has this happened before?
2. Are you in love with Emma?
3. When was the last time this happened to you?
4. Is she in love with you?
5. Are you afraid of girls hurting you or you hurting them?

Now turn all five closed questions into open questions.

Open questions – case study 2 – Amanda

Amanda says, 'I don't know what to do. My husband is going out to America on contract. Charles wants me to go with him, but I'm afraid. I've never been away from this country. If I stay here I can carry on working and earn some extra money which we desperately need. But if I don't go, I shan't see him for months on end. What should I do?'

Here are five closed questions:

1.   What part of America?
2.   How long will he be away for?
3.   You're afraid of going, aren't you?
4.   How much money will you be able to earn while he's away?
5.   What sort of work does Charles do?

Now turn all five closed questions into open questions.

This is the end of the open questions exercises. When you have reformatted all the questions turn to Appendix 2 for suggested responses.

Exercise 9

Summarising – case study 1 – Tom

Tom says, 'Now don't you start Andy. I had enough of that with my old man when he was alive, never forgave me for letting the side down. I can hear him now, going on and on, "All our family have gone to the grammar school and have all done well, we want to be proud of you too." What a load of rubbish! I'd had enough of school. I suppose I'm the black sheep. The only child, and what have I got to be proud of?'

Identify the key words, then construct a brief summary.

Summarising – case study 2 – Tom

Tom says, 'A bastard, that's what I am, Andy. All right, in law I'm not, but that's what I am, a bastard, bastard, bastard. God, what a mess. You know how I found out? When I was 15, mother and the old man were having one of their endless rows one night. I was in the attic doing some experiment, my workshop was up there; I think they'd forgotten me. I heard the old man shout at her. "I suppose you've got another fancy man, and then I'll have to take his child as mine, just like I did Tom." I couldn't hear any more, the door was slammed.'

Identify the key words, then construct a brief summary.

This is the end of the summarising exercises. Turn to Appendix 2 for suggested responses.

Exercise 10

Focusing – case study – Sally

Sally, 20, a student nurse, is speaking to the college counsellor: 'I'm in a mess. I moved out of the hospital residence six months ago into a house with four other students, several miles from the college, so I had to buy a car. Two of the others have moved on since then, and the two new ones are awful. They leave the kitchen like a pigsty, and we have endless rows. The atmosphere is so unpleasant. Plus the fact that they're so noisy, playing loud music and banging doors.

A month ago I had a prang with the car, when it was standing outside in the street. I've only got third party, so I couldn't claim on the insurance, and it's going to cost a bomb to repair. I'm already badly overdrawn and the bank keep writing to me. They take off so much when my pay cheque goes in that I barely have enough to live on. In fact I eat so badly that I'm losing weight like an anorexic. To crown it all, my last assignment at college was awful. They made me resit, and I can't find the energy to even start it. What am I going to do?'

1. Formulate a contrast response to Sally.
2. Formulate a choice-point response to Sally.
3. Formulate a figure-ground response to Sally.

This is the end of the focusing exercises. Turn to Appendix 2 for suggested responses.

Exercise 11

Being concrete

In these exercises you are asked to turn a generalised, vague statement into a concrete one.

The aim of these exercises is a three-fold one:

1. To help you when a client is making a concrete or generalised statement.
2. To help you make more concrete than generalised statements.
3. To enable you, through being more concrete, to help clients explore their situation more effectively.

Case study 1 – Adam, generalised and vague

Adam says, 'I'm not very considerate to my wife.'

Imagine you are Adam. What sort of things would you say that would tell the listener precisely just how you relate to your wife?

Case study 2 – Judith, generalised and vague

Judith says, 'I find these counselling training groups really difficult.'

Imagine you are Judith. What sort of things would you say that would tell the listener precisely just what your difficulties are?

Case study 3 – Bill, generalised and vague

Bill says, 'I feel uneasy about the relationship with my mother.'

Imagine you are Bill. What sort of things would you say that would tell the listener precisely your feelings about your mother?

This is the end of the being concrete exercises. Turn to Appendix 2 for suggested responses.

Summary

In this chapter we have:

◆ explored primary level empathy
◆ related empathy to the skill of active listening
◆ explored some of the basic listening skills, which are no more than effective communications skills
◆ demonstrated through case studies how these skills can be used effectively.

The basic active listening skills discussed in this chapter pave the way for other listening skills which require more experience and advanced empathy; which takes listening to surface and stated feelings to what lies underneath; to what is implied.

In helping others, we shall help ourselves,
for whatever good we give out completes
the circle and comes back to us.

Flora Edwards

*Counselling
facilitates client
understanding
of the situation
in order to move
forward.*

CHAPTER 5

Helping the Client Understand the Problem

*There is no challenge more challenging
than the challenge to improve yourself.*

Michael F. Staley

Using the basic active listening skills may take the client some way along the path of self-awareness, yet more may be needed to help the client gain a deeper understanding of the problem and its root cause. In this chapter we provide insight into the skills the counsellor uses to facilitate understanding. These skills, unfortunately termed 'challenging and confronting', invite clients to examine their behaviour and its consequences. In other words, by encouraging the client to come face-to-face with herself, she develops the skill of self-challenge and the potential to change. However, it needs to be borne in mind that in the context of counselling, challenges and confrontations are always offered with the client's best interests at heart – as a gift, not an attack. The skills need to be used with great sensitivity, care and respect. They need to come out of a deep empathy with the client, and should not be used until trust has been well established.

Challenging and confronting

The aim of challenging is to provide accurate information and to offer our perspective. We challenge the strengths of the client rather than the weaknesses – we point out the strengths, assets and resources which the client may fail to fully use. Challenging and confronting helps clients develop new perspectives. Figure 18 gives an overview of the skills the counsellor uses to facilitate understanding on the problem. The skills covered in this section are specific to challenging.

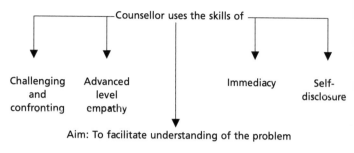

Fig. 18. An overview of the skills the counsellor uses
to facilitate understanding of the problem.

Confronting a client

Many people get the misguided image of counsellors as a
bunch of head nodders or do-gooders, who get paid a lot of
money for just sitting and listening. Confronting a client with
something she might prefer not to see, might not want to hear
or might not want to know, is not easy. It can be a painful
learning process for the client, as well as a risky business for
the counsellor. It takes guts to challenge a client, and the
counsellor may well be left wondering whether she has said the
right thing. It can also be an exhausting experience for both.

What confrontation is and is not

◆ Confrontation is not verbal fisticuffs or a head-on clash!
◆ Confrontation should be a tentative suggestion, not a
  declaration.
◆ Confrontation is an observation, not an accusation.
◆ Confrontation should be made only after careful
  deliberation.
◆ Confrontation should never be used as retaliation or a put
  down.
◆ Confrontation is safest when the relationship is well
  established.

The main areas of confrontation are:

1. Discrepancies, distortions and manipulations.
2. Negative thought patterns and behaviours.
3. Games, tricks and smoke screens.
4. Excuses: manipulation, complacency, rationalisations,
   procrastinations, passing the buck.

Forms of confronting:

1. 'Your perspective is ... mine ... is'
2. 'When you say/do ... I think/feel ... '
3. 'On the one hand you are saying ... on the other you are saying ... '
4. 'You have said (or done) ... my reaction is ... '

Examples of confrontations

Discrepancy

◆ 'You say that being rejected has really upset you, yet you smile as you talk about it.'

◆ 'When you arrived, I observed a smiling and happy-go-lucky person sitting opposite me, and yet this doesn't seem to fit with the words I am hearing.'

◆ 'On the one hand you say you love your wife, but on the other you say you have a mistress.'

◆ 'You have mentioned to me several times that you hate arriving late for appointments, yet I've noticed that you have been late for the last two sessions, and I'm wondering what that's about.'

◆ 'You speak of your many losses, yet you smile continuously.'

◆ 'You say you are fine, yet you seem to be very close to tears.'

Distortion of feelings

◆ 'You say you feel really depressed, yet you laugh whenever you say that, as if it was nothing at all.'

◆ 'You say you are not worried about your exams, yet you are spending all your evenings in the students' bar drowning your sorrows.'

◆ 'You say you feel lonely, yet you shrug it off as though it's not important.'

Manipulation

◆ 'You say your parents have never really understood you. However, the way you said that makes me wonder if you are trying to play on my sympathy in some way.'

◆ 'You know you have the ability to pass your first year finals, yet you say you haven't bothered to write up your assignments. You are hoping that I can bail you out of this tricky situation by having a word with your tutor.'

Negative thought patterns

◆ 'You say that you don't think you are up to handling this change in your life. Yet you are clearly a resourceful person. You're intelligent and motivated and have coped well with changes in the past.'
◆ 'You say you are finding it difficult to decide whether you should accept this new job. Yet from other things you have told me, you strike me as a person who normally finds it easy to make decisions.'

Excuses

◆ 'You say you believe in taking responsibility for what you do, yet I hear you blaming your wife and daughter for everything that is wrong in your relationship with them.'
◆ 'You say you want to go back to college, and yet it feels as though you are putting obstacles in the way when I hear you keep saying: "Yes but ...".'
◆ 'You say you are keen to apply for a new job, yet you seem reluctant to update your CV.'

Complacency

◆ 'You say you've been out of work for six months, and it really gets you down. Yet in all that time you haven't applied for any jobs, and you're quite happy to collect your money every week; "That's what I've paid in for all these years!" you said.'
◆ 'You say you would like a better relationship with your wife. Yet for the past six months you have been going out almost every evening with the lads.'

Procrastination

◆ 'A month ago you moaned because you hadn't worked for

six months. You made a contract then to start looking for work, now you're telling me you haven't even tried. You haven't kept your contract, and didn't realise how the time was flying.'

♦ 'In our fifth session, you told me how desperate you were to give up smoking, and you had joined a "smoke stop" group. Yet now you are telling me that you haven't attended for the past three weeks.'

Rationalisation

♦ 'Last time you admitted that you kept putting off looking for a job, now you're saying you couldn't go because the weather was wet.'

♦ 'In the last group session you told us all you wanted to settle down with your partner, now you're saying you want to sow a few wild oats.'

Effective confrontation

A confrontation should be preceded by careful consideration:
1. What is the purpose of the confrontation?
2. Can I handle the consequences?
3. Does the confrontation relate to the here and now?
4. Whose needs are being met by the confrontation?

Effective confrontation usually contains elements of some or all of the following:
1. A reflection or summary of what the client has said so that the client feels heard and understood.
2. A statement of the counsellor's present feelings.
3. A concrete statement of what the counsellor has noticed or observed, given without interpretation.

Examples of confronting

1. *Client:*
   Jane says, 'I don't know what's wrong with me; I can never seem to get to work on time. Not only am I late, but often I'm so tired I can't get up. Evenings are all right, though. I go to church every evening, and most nights I'm with the

team around the down-and-outs of the city. I really enjoy that, and somehow I don't feel tired.'

Counsellor:
'Jane, you obviously have an absorbing passion for the down-and-outs and this takes you out pretty late, yet you often have trouble getting to work on time. I wonder if there a discrepancy somewhere there, between responsibility to your employer and your charitable works.'

2. *Group member:*
    Albert says, 'What's the matter with me? I sit here in this training group, week after week and wonder what I'm getting out of it, or if I've anything to give. It's so frustrating. I have plenty to say, but nobody seems to want to listen.'

    Group leader:
    'Albert, I hear your frustration, you want to say something in the group, you feel you have plenty to say yet you merge into the background like the wallpaper, as if you wanted to make yourself invisible. When you've taken your courage in both hands and spoken out, I've appreciated what you've said, usually to the point of the discussion, as if you've given it a lot of thought. Yet there are many other times when you have tried to speak, and your voice has been so soft, as if you were apologising for speaking.'

3. *Clive (looking tearful):*
    'I've failed my finals, but I don't really care. My good social life makes up for all that, and I can try again in three months' time. Maybe if I don't make it I could try something else. What do you think?'

    Counsellor:
    'Clive, on the one hand you are saying you don't care that you've failed your finals, but you look very downhearted. You think you could try something else, yet you want to have another crack at the finals in three months. What do you think about these discrepancies?

Examples of effective confrontation

Let us resume with the five clients, Pat, Paul, Claire, Ellen and Danny again, to see how the counsellor might use confrontation.

Pat

Counsellor to Pat: 'Pat, when I hear you talking about being raped, you appear very calm. However, this doesn't seem to fit with your body-language, which seems to be saying how desperate you really feel.'

Paul:
Counsellor to Paul: 'Paul, you say that you desperately want to get a job, however, you then tell me that you have given up trying. There seems to be a contradiction here.'

Claire:
Counsellor to Claire: 'Claire, you say that you feel absolutely useless and this is what makes you hurt yourself, yet just now you told me that you had got a place at university, which seems to contradict your view of yourself.'

Ellen:
Counsellor to Ellen: 'Ellen, on the one hand you say that the idea of sharing your life with Peter appeals to you, and on the other that you would feel guilty because you think you would be letting Charlie down. There seems to be a discrepancy between your wanting to remain loyal to Charlie and wanting to have a new life with Peter.'

Danny:
Counsellor to Danny: 'Danny, you say that you don't think it's alcohol that makes you aggressive, and yet you have told me that you are a different person when you haven't been drinking.'

Using advanced level empathy

Advanced level empathy works more (but not exclusively) with implied feelings – those that lie below the surface – and hunches. The aim is to help clients see their problems and concerns more clearly and in a context that will enable them to move forward.

Hunches can be communicated as follows:

To get a larger picture

'It seems that the problem is not only in the relationship between you and the charge nurse; it looks as if the war between you has spread to the rest of the team.'

'I've noticed recently that when you talk about your feelings you seem to somehow cushion them. For example, today you said that you got a "*teeny bit*" annoyed with..., you were "*quite*" upset with..., you feel "*pretty*" anxious about... I've got a hunch that maybe cushioning your feelings serves a very important purpose for you...'

To challenge indirect expression or implication

'What I think I'm hearing is that it's more than disappointment about the end of the friendship, perhaps it's also about pain and anger.'

To draw logical conclusions

'From what you say about the charge nurse, although you haven't actually used the word, I wonder if you're feeling bitter towards him.'

To challenge hints

'Several times over about the last three sessions, you've brought up relationships with men, though you haven't pursued them, although the door was left open for you. My hunch is that sexual relationships is an important subject, yet you find it difficult to address it.'

To challenge blind spots

'I wonder if the way you laugh at serious things give some people the impression of an attitude of not caring and of being cynical.'

'I'm wondering if you realise that when you talk about your grandfather your face radiates warmth and you become animated, yet when you mention your father your face goes pale, your voice goes quiet, and you almost seem to shrink in size...'

To identify themes

'Several times you've mentioned certain things about women. I wonder if underlying that points to an attitude that puts women down. For example, you said, "I don't think women drivers are as reliable as men". Then you said... "What do you think about that?"'

To own thoughts

'My hunch is that you've already decided to pack that job in, though you haven't said so in so many words.'

The ability to identify implied feelings is closely linked to intuition and imagination. For many of us, however, the imagination and intuition we were born with have been overlaid by thinking and sensing activities. Careful nurturing and use will help them to resurface.

Example 1 – advanced level empathy – Susan to her friend Mandy

'Just listen to us. We're both talking, but we're not really listening, I mean. Are we all so self-centred that we can't take time to listen to each other?'

Identified feelings: Angry, disappointed, furious, ready to explode, ready to pull out, ready to wash your hands of the whole group.

Mandy says: 'Susan, I hear your anger coming from a long way down, as if you've been keeping it in check for some time, and even now you don't really want to let it out in case someone gets hurt. I also sense that tied up with the anger is an intense disappointment which is almost pushing you out of the group, because we are not listening to your needs.'

Example 2 – advanced level empathy – John talking with Dave, his teenage son

John says: 'Dave, we've been fighting each other for years, not listening to each other, pushing our own views and competing with each other. Today, it's like we've really talked. And you know, Dave, it's been great talking with you rather than at you. Maybe I've been afraid of that.'

Identified feelings: Achieved something, at peace, fulfilled, load taken off, moving closer, new ground, relief, satisfied.

Dave says: 'Dad, it seems as if you and I have been talking at each other from different planets, or from different sides of the earth. Now we're talking face-to-face, man-to-man, and that feels good. It's as if we've both won a tremendous victory, and now you feel we can work hard at establishing peace between us.'

Example 3 – advanced level empathy – George

This example uses the situation in Example 1 of primary level where George is talking to his counsellor about his girlfriend, Jenny, and says: 'I keep telling myself not to move too quickly with Jenny. She's so quiet, and when she does say anything, it' usually how nervous she is. It's obvious to me that when I say anything to her she gets fidgety and anxious, then I wish I hadn't opened my mouth. It's like a checkmate. If I move I push her away, and if I don't move, nothing will happen between us, and I'll lose her anyway.'

Identified feelings: Anxious, Catch-22, cautious, frustrated, protective, regret.

Counsellor says: 'George, it seems that you feel quite frustrated that things are not developing with Jenny as quickly as you would like, and that there's something in the relationship that makes you both back off. Yet I also sense that you feel there's something about you that puts her off, and that maybe you feel things will never come to anything, and yet you feel trapped somehow and not able to let go.'

Forms of advanced empathic responding:
◆ 'I can sense that you feel...'
◆ 'I have this hunch that...'
◆ 'The picture I am getting...'
◆ 'I have a fantasy that...'
◆ 'The image I am getting is one of...'
◆ 'I imagine you...'
◆ 'I guess it's as if...'
◆ 'My gut feeling is...'

When formulating advanced empathic responses it must be remembered that implied facts and feelings are never stated as absolutes; they are hunches, and as such they must be tentative.

Examples of advanced empathy

Let's pick up again with Pat, Paul, Claire, Ellen and Danny and see how the counsellor might use advanced empathy.

Pat:
Counsellor to Pat: 'Pat, I can sense that you feel very distraught about what has happened, and you seem to be holding on to a lot of pain.' *(Pat bursts into tears.)*

Paul:
Counsellor to Paul: 'Paul, I have a hunch I would like to share with you. I somehow get a picture of someone who is struggling to keep his head above water, but the setbacks he keeps getting leave him feeling as if he's beginning to drown in a sea of despair.'

Claire:
Counsellor to Claire: 'Claire, the image I am getting is of someone who has lost all hope of ever being able to stop

harming herself. It's as if she feels so useless that she deserves to be punished in some way.'

Ellen:

Counsellor to Ellen: 'Ellen, the picture I am getting is like a photograph that has been torn in two. In one part of the photograph I see a woman who is filled with hope because she has found a man she would like to share her life with. However, the other part shows a very different story. In this part I see a woman who is filled with confusion and ... perhaps ... guilt ... because she feels as if she is being unfaithful to her beloved Charlie by even considering the idea of sharing her life with another man. It feels to me as if she's in a no win situation – like there is no way she can see how the two torn pieces can ever be repaired.'

Danny

Counsellor to Danny: 'Danny, the image I am getting is of a young man who perhaps lacks self-confidence, and who uses drink to give himself Dutch courage to join in, and perhaps to be accepted by his mates? But when he drinks it seems to completely change his character from a person who is usually quiet and inoffensive, to a person who is loud, punchy and aggressive – a bit like Jekyll and Hyde. I somehow sense that the quiet Danny feels embarrassed and ashamed by the behaviour of the loud and aggressive Danny, and quiet Danny would like to be able to control loud Danny's unacceptable behaviour.'

Using immediacy as a way of discussing your relationship with the client

Immediacy is about open and honest communication. It's about being aware of what is happening in the counselling relationship at any given moment, and reflecting this back to the client tentatively and sensitively. Immediacy can be defined as the skill of discussing your relationship with your clients, and is also referred to as 'here and now', or 'you–me talk'. The aim of immediacy is to address lack of direction that might be having a bearing on the relationship, any tension experienced between client and counsellor, lack of trust, attraction and dependency or counter-dependency. Immediacy makes it possible for both client and counsellor to see more clearly what is going on between them. Immediacy includes perceiving what is happening and putting it into words, putting yourself on the spot about your own and the client's feelings, and pointing out distortions, games and discrepancies which are going on in the counselling room – in the relationship – in the 'here and now'. It helps the client look at the interaction within the relationship, as it is happening.

Clients often talk about feelings in the past (the then and there), rather than in the 'now'. They also have a tendency to act (or 'act out') the very behaviours and feelings with which they have expressed having difficulty. They may try to set the counsellor up with the kind of relationships that are causing them difficulties in their everyday lives. Immediacy enables the counsellor to highlight these interactions.

People who rarely talk in the present often dilute the interactions by the use of 'you' instead of 'I'. Clients may be helped to feel the immediacy of the statement when 'I' is used.

Examples of immediacy

♦ 'You say that you have never been able to talk to your mother, and I wonder if you realise that whenever we start to discuss painful concerns, you give me warning signals to back off?'

♦ 'I would like us to stop for a moment and see what is happening between us. We have talked freely so far, but now we seem to have reached a kind of "stuckness" which is leaving me feeling quite tense. I wonder if you share my feeling?'

♦ 'I find it difficult, listening to you, to know how you really feel right now. You talk about everything as if you were talking about somebody else. How do you feel about what I've just said?'

♦ 'When you talk about your employees, you sound as if you're talking about little children. Just now you used the same tone with me. I felt really very small and put down. How do you feel about me saying that?'

◆ 'When you were telling me about being burgled, you looked so calm yet I felt a great surge of anger within me. I wonder was that my anger, or was I picking up your hidden anger?'

◆ 'I just want to tell you that right now I'm feeling irritated. Whenever we start to talk about your relationship with your wife you clam up, cross your legs and fold your arms, which tell me to 'keep out', and I'm finding that frustrating. I'm wondering if that is how your wife feels when she tries to talk to you?'

Counsellors cannot change a third person, and cannot change a client. What counsellors can do is help clients to change themselves, and this can influence the relationship with third persons in a way that is most constructive. The relationship between counsellor and client therefore becomes a model, and an environment for testing out new behaviours.

As with confronting a client, and advanced empathy, immediacy is more appropriate when the counselling relationship is firmly established. As concreteness contrasts with generality, so here-and-now immediacy contrasts with 'then and there'. The principal difference is that in the one, clients are encouraged to own their feelings and not to generalise; in the other, they are encouraged to own their feelings as they exist *at that moment*.

Examples of using immediacy

Let us see now how a counsellor might use immediacy with our five clients, Pat, Paul, Claire, Ellen and Danny.

Pat:
Counsellor to Pat: 'Pat, I see you smiling when you talk about being raped, and yet I feel enraged. I'm not too sure where that rage is coming from, but I wonder if I could be picking up the real feeling behind your smile?'

Paul:
Counsellor to Paul: 'Paul, when you talk about not being successful with getting a job, you sound pretty angry and as if you want to blame someone. It feels right now as if I am the target of your anger, like you want to blame me in some way.'

Claire:

Counsellor to Claire: 'Claire, when you were telling me about how you cut and burn yourself, I felt quite helpless and inadequate. It felt almost like you expected me to provide an instant cure, and because I can't come up with one, I've disappointed you. How do you feel about me saying this?'

Ellen:

Counsellor to Ellen: 'Ellen, when you talked about the habits Charlie had that irritated you, I felt really uncomfortable, and I'm not sure what this is all about. I wonder if I am picking up this feeling from you – like it somehow feels wrong to speak ill of the dead?'

Danny:

Counsellor to Danny: 'Danny, when you talk about your relationship with your father, I wonder if you realise that your voice gets louder, you clench your fists, and your knuckles go white. I'm feeling a bit threatened by it, and I wonder if that's how your father feels when he tries to have a discussion with you.'

What immediacy involves:

1. Being open with the client about how you feel about something in the relationship.
2. Disclosing a hunch about the client's behaviour towards you by drawing attention to discrepancies, distortions, avoidances, games.
3. Inviting the client to explore what is happening, with a view to developing a more productive working relationship.

Disclosing self to facilitate communication

Immediacy and disclosing self often go hand in hand. Frequently it is the disclosure of a behaviour or feeling by the counsellor which starts this way of communicating. A strategy for disclosing self is to use 'I' statements: 'I sense that ...' or I feel that ...', rather than 'you said ...' or 'you did'. By using 'I' statements the client is not attacked, and can respond appropriately, either denying or accepting that she feels the same way. It can also encourage the client to use 'I' statements and thus take responsibility for their own thoughts, feelings and behaviour.

Disclosing self is the process by which we let ourselves be known to others, and, in the process, we enhance our self-awareness. Disclosing self means that the counsellor makes a conscious decision to reveal something to the client. Essentially it means we share with the client a similar experience to the one that is causing her present difficulties, and use the common denominator to work with.

Disclosing self is only useful if it encourages the client to self-disclose and open herself up to the counselling process. Accurately used, disclosing self can be helpful and positive, but inappropriate and mistimed disclosures may increase the client's anxiety, particularly where it shifts the emphasis from the client to the counsellor. The client comes with her own set of problems, and it doesn't help her to know what problems the counsellor has. Another danger of disclosing self is the impression that it may give of 'If I have overcome it ...' or 'This is the way I overcame it ...' , the implication being that the client can do the same.

> *Disclosing self must be used with caution and discretion.*

Disclosing self is only appropriate if:

1. It keeps the client on target and doesn't distract.
2. It does not add to the client's burden.
3. It is not done too often.

Recognising appropriate disclosures

Appropriate disclosures involve sharing of:
◆ attitudes
◆ beliefs
◆ feelings
◆ reactions to the client
◆ views.

Disclosures should be:

- ◆ direct
- ◆ sensitive
- ◆ relevant
- ◆ non-possessive
- ◆ brief
- ◆ selective.

Reasons for disclosing self

1. Using self as a model.
2. Showing genuineness in helping.
3. Sharing experiences.
4. Sharing feelings.
5. Sharing opinions.
6. Modelling assertiveness.

Not all counsellors agree with disclosing self. It is embraced in humanistic therapies, but seldom in psychodynamic therapies, where it is believed that to disclose self can get in the way of constructive counselling.

Examples of disclosing self:

1. Peter was talking to Roy about his father's recent death. Peter was having difficulty expressing himself until Roy said, 'My father died four years after my mother. When he died I felt I'd been orphaned. Maybe that is something like how you feel.' Peter sat for several minutes in deep silence before saying, 'You've put into words exactly how I feel. May I talk about my childhood and how Dad and I got on together?'

2. Janet, a nurse, was working with Sheila, one of her patients, when Sheila said, 'Janet, you're very quiet today, and seem on edge, have I upset you in some way?' Janet said, 'Sorry, Sheila, it's not you. Simon and I had an argument before we left for work, and it's still on my mind. Thank you for drawing my attention to it. My feelings could easily have got in the way with you and others. Let's think about you, now.' Having made this disclosure, Janet moves on and returns the focus to the client.

Disclosing self – important points to remember

◆ Although counsellors should be willing to make disclosures about themselves that might help clients understand some part of their problem more clearly, they should do so only such disclosures do not disturb or distract the clients in their own work.

◆ Disclosing self is more appropriate in well established relationships, and should reflect the needs of the client, not the needs of the counsellor.

Examples of using self-disclosure

Let us return now to our five clients, Pat, Paul, Claire, Ellen and Danny, and see how a counsellor might use self-disclosure to reflect the needs of the client.

Pat:

Counsellor to Pat: 'Pat, I would like to share something with yo if you don't mind? I was raped when I was 15, and I can remember feeling dirty and contaminated. I also blamed myself because I felt I should have tried harder to stop him. I wonder if that's anywhere close to how you are feeling right now?'

Paul:

Counsellor to Paul: 'Paul, when you talked about all the application forms you have sent off, it took me back to when my job was made redundant. I can remember sending off load of application forms, and feeling very rejected when I didn't get any replies. It nearly destroyed my self-confidence. I wonde if you can identify with any of those feelings I experienced?'

Claire:

Counsellor to Claire: 'Claire, would you mind if I shared something with you? When I was a teenager I was fat, and I used to get called horrible names at school. I'll never forget them because they hurt so much – names like "ugly", "grotesque", "fatso", "freak". I heard these names so often that ended up believing that I was some sort of worthless monster, who should be annihilated. I wanted to murder the kids who said it, and then I felt guilty for having such evil thoughts. I hated myself so much I just wanted to die. I wonder whether you can relate to any of those feelings I experienced?'

Ellen:
Counsellor to Ellen: 'Ellen, I can remember feeling incredibly guilty when I formed a new relationship two years after my husband had died. It felt almost as if I was having an affair behind his back and that left me feeling as if I had betrayed his trust in me. I wonder if you are carrying around any feelings similar to those I had?'

Danny:
Counsellor to Danny: 'Danny, when I was about your age I had a scrape or two with the law. Each time it was when I'd had one over the eight, which made me boisterous and rowdy. I remember thumping my mate once because he'd been chatting my girlfriend up, and then feeling terribly guilty, remorseful and ashamed of myself when I sobered up and realised what I'd done. I wonder if any of those feelings I experienced are ringing bells with you.'

Counsellor self-disclosure is only helpful if it:
◆ keeps the client on target
◆ serves the needs of the client
◆ moves the client forward to self-understanding.

It should be used with tact and sensitivity and only when a relationship of trust has been established between client and counsellor.

Exercises

Exercise 12: confronting a client

Your task is to create a confrontation response to each of the following case studies.

Case study 1 – Vanessa
Vanessa says, 'I do wish I could do something about my

weight. Look at me, 15 stones. But, I'm my own worst enemy. Stuart and I went out last night for a slap-up meal. That's the way of it. One of these days I'll win, though.'

How would you confront Vanessa?

Case study 2 – Dan

Dan says, 'I don't have any problems with my children, we have a wonderful relationship, that's because Alice and I give them responsibility. They know who's boss, though. Bill wanted a front door key. I told him, "When you're working, my lad, then you can have a key to my house. You're only 17 yet." He stormed out, muttering something like, "Come into this century, old man." Cheeky young (cough).'

How would you confront Dan?

We can also use confrontations to bring out strengths of which the client seems unaware, or is discounting. This is, of course, a discrepancy, but of a different kind.

Case study 3 – Keith

Keith was about to be demobbed from the army, in which he had served for 22 years. He was a sergeant with an exemplary record. He had served in Northern Ireland on two tours, and had been decorated for bravery. One of his duties, for four years, had been in charge of the sergeants' mess accounts, a job that carried a lot of financial responsibility. He and Mavis married 19 years ago. She had been in the WRAC. They have two boys, Adrian, aged 18, and John, aged 17, both in the army. They have a stable family life, with both sets of parents still alive.

On his pre-release interview he said to the interviewing officer, 'I'm scared stiff, Sir, of going back into Civvy Street. I've been in the army since I was 18, and boys' service before that, so I've never known anything else since 16. I married an army girl, and we've lived in army quarters all our married life. Our two boys are in the services. I don't know anything else. When I think about it, I get cold sweats. I'm not sleeping well either, just thinking about it.'

How would you confront Keith?

This is the end of the confronting exercises. Turn to Appendix 2 for suggested responses.

Exercise 13: *identifying your own strengths*

Have a dialogue with yourself. Talk about your strengths. Be realistic, not coy. Many people have difficulty even saying they have strengths. Part of your self-development as a counsellor is discovering how you feel about drawing attention to your strong points. Many people are happier talking about their weaknesses and hardly ever realise that they have strengths. Counselling is often concerned with identifying strengths and building on them. The client can no more build on weaknesses than a builder can build a house on a foundation of sand. When you have considered your strengths, write them down in your notebook. Try to list at least five.

Exercise 14: *advanced empathy*

This is a suggested framework on how to formulate responses for the advanced empathy case study exercises.

Read the case studies and identify the expressed facts and feelings and the implied facts and feelings. When you have done this, think of what those facts and feelings might imply. When you have done this, think of as many adjectives as you can to describe the implied feelings, then formulate your response. Remember, implied facts and feelings are never stated as absolutes; they are hunches, and as such they must be tentative.

Case study 1 – Nigel to Brenda, a counsellor

'You know me, Brenda, the life and soul of the party. Give me a pint in my hand and I'll keep them amused for hours. It's not like that in the house, though. "Oh, shut up Dad," is all I get. "Don't put on that act here. Be your age." It hurts. Sometimes they get quite angry at my jokes. Why don't they appreciate me?'

Create a response of about six to eight lines.

Case study 2 – Kate, a senior nurse teacher, talking to Simon, a colleague

'It's no secret, and you know better than anybody else, I'm a workaholic. I can't remember when I allowed myself to have a day off to do just nothing. It sounds awful when it's put like that. I've been that way for 12 years now. I ought to do something about it, shouldn't I? I'm a free agent. Nobody's making me do it, or holding a gun to my head. I feel caught on a treadmill.'

Create a response of about six to eight lines.

Case study 3 – Karen, talking to Joan, one of the counsellors in attendance at the church coffee morning

I love Jack and my children very much, and I like doing most things around the house. Of course they get boring at times, but on the whole I suppose it can be very rewarding sometimes. I don't really miss working, going to the office every day. Most women complain of being just a housewife and just a mother. But then, again, I wonder if there's more for me. Others say there has to be. I really don't know.'

Create a response of about eight to ten lines.

In the above exercise and the next one, you will not be given an analysis. When you compare your response with the one given, see if you can identify why Joan responds the way she does.

Case study 4 – Andrea's fourth counselling session with Martin

Andrea says: 'I'm really disappointed in you, Martin. I thought we could get along together and you could help me. But we're not getting anywhere. You don't understand me. I might as well not be here. I don't even think you care for me, and you don't hear me when I talk. You seem to be somewhere else. What you say has got nothing to do with what I've been talking about. I don't know where to turn. I'm just so – oh damn it – I don't know what I'm going to do, but I know you can't help me. There's no hope.'

Create a response of about eight to ten lines.

This is the end of the advanced empathy exercises. Turn to
Appendix 2 for suggested responses.

Exercise 15: immediacy

In these case study exercises, use the following formula:
- disclose specifically how the issue affects you
- create a specific empathic challenge
- as with a challenge, immediacy should be tentative – an
  invitation to consider.

Case study 1 – Alan

You are a facilitator of a counselling training group of twelve
people. One of the group, Alan, is very vocal, and always seems
to have an answer to any point that you or anyone else raises. In
the third session, you start to feel irritated. The source of your
irritation is that whenever silences occur, Alan invariably jumps
in with a comment that does not always facilitate what has gone
before. You also notice that other members of the group start to
fidget and cast knowing glances at one another when Alan starts
speaking. The immediate issue is that Alan cuts across what one
of the women in the group is saying. What do you say to Alan?

Create a response to Alan.

Case study 2 – Jenny

You are a member of a counselling group. There has been a lot of
disclosure and some tears. Cathy is talking about the pain of her
recent divorce. Many people in the group are looking damp-eyed.
Jenny gets up and walks right through the middle of the group to
the door, saying, 'I need a smoke'. The group members look
very uncomfortable. After a few minutes, Jenny recrosses the
group and sits down. As a member of the group you feel angry at
what you feel is an intrusion. What do you say to Jenny?

Create a response to Jenny.

Case study 3 – Steve

Steve is your client, and this is the sixth session. When he
started with you, he said, 'Oh, I'm fairly well off, so the fee

isn't a problem.' You, personally, have difficulty talking about charging a fee, you would much rather leave that to someone else to handle, but there is no one else. At least three times during your time together, Steve has said things like, 'I hadn't realised just how expensive this business would be'. You find that this issue is unresolved. You also wonder if Steve thinks that the length of the counselling relationship is more to do with your needs than with his.

Create a response to Steve.

Case study 4 – Sally

Sally, aged 19, is a student at the college where you are the counsellor. She came to you six months ago, referred by her lecturer, for problems with relationships in the group. She came regularly, every week, for six weeks, then started missing sessions altogether. Your policy is to drop a line after one missed appointment expressing concern and hoping that illness or an emergency did not prevent her from attending.

You also remind her of the next agreed appointment. Usually she would attend the next appointment, with apologies, which sounded like excuses rather than reasons. Several times you have challenged her on this unreliability and on every occasion she says, 'I really, really promise to do better'. She had a break from counselling for two months, and one month ago started again. She came for two sessions, missed one and is now sitting with you. She says, in a pleading little-girl voice, 'I'm really, really sorry. Can you forgive me?'

Create a response to Sally.

This is the end of the immediacy case study exercises. Turn to Appendix 2 for suggested responses.

Exercise 16: unfinished business

Think of someone you have 'unfinished business' with that you would like to resolve.

1. Describe the current situation.
2. What are your thoughts about this person? Try to identify both positive and negative thoughts.

3.   What are your feelings about this person? Try to identify both positive and negative feelings.

4.   Endeavour to put yourself in this person's shoes, and explore why you think the person is treating you the way he/she is.

5.   What could you say to this person to encourage her or him to discuss the unresolved issue?

6.   Look carefully at your response to number 5, and consider whether you could pluck up the courage to say this to the person concerned.

Exercise 17

Disclosing self: 1

Disclosure of self is different from previous exercises, and is clearly linked to the development of self-awareness. It would be difficult to present an exercise on disclosing self to which every student could respond appropriately, for disclosing self is so uniquely personal. The object of this exercise is that you think around some aspect of living which you feel you have handled reasonably well, or are learning to manage. Remember, the aim of disclosing self is to help the client to move forward, not to pass problems on to the client. To help you, here are some ideas. What could you disclose and to whom? You may choose any other subject or subjects.

There are no suggested responses to this exercise.

What are your views, feelings and thoughts about:
◆   Religious groups other than your own.
◆   Your experience of drinking, smoking, drugs.
◆   Your sexual preferences.
◆   Your childhood experiences.
◆   Your feelings about the client you are counselling.
◆   How much you are worth financially.
◆   The aspects of your personality you are not happy with.
◆   Things in the past you are ashamed of.
◆   The sort of things that can hurt you.
◆   The parts of your body you don't like.
◆   Whether or not you feel sexually adequate.

Disclosing self: 2

For this exercise enlist the help of a friend. Role-play being a counsellor, with your friend taking the part of the client. Ask your friend to talk about something important to him or her for 15 minutes. During this time, make several personal disclosures and talk about your experiences.

At the end of the 15 minutes ask your partner for feedback on the impact of your personal disclosures, eg:

◆ Did your personal disclosures help or hinder your friend? In what way?

◆ Did your personal disclosures distract your friend?

Summary

It might be helpful at this point in the book to summarise our journey so far. We have:

◆ provided insight into what counselling is, and what defines a counsellor

◆ explored counsellor qualities deemed necessary to work effectively with others, and provided opportunities for increasing self-awareness

◆ given consideration to boundary issues and provided information on what counsellors can do to help their clients feel safe

◆ presented a range of basic listening skills and advanced skills, with exercises designed to develop the skills.

We are almost on the homeward strait, but there's still a few more important topics we need to pay attention to, the next being: What can counsellors do to help their clients resolve their problems?

> *The possibility of encountering one's reality –*
> *learning about one's self – can be frightening and frustrating.*
> *Many people expect to discover the worst.*
> *A hidden fear lies in the fact that they may also discover the best.*
> Muriel James and Dorothy Jongeward

CHAPTER 6

Helping the Client Resolve the Problem

*There comes a moment when you have to stop revving up
the car and shove it into gear.*

David Mahoney

We have stressed throughout this book that counselling is about change. However, it's important to recognise that some things cannot be changed. Just as we cannot alter the colour of our eyes or our height, we cannot reverse incurable illness or a physical disability. We cannot give a one-legged man two limbs, or a blind person sight. What counsellors can do in these circumstances is to offer help and support in coming to terms with what cannot be changed, and encouragement to explore strategies for coping with the situation.

Up until now, emphasis has been placed on the value of good communication in the counselling relationship. Yet there comes a time when talking may not be enough and the client needs to take the bull by the horns and *do* something. Put another way, he or she needs to take action to resolve the problem. To this end, the counsellor can play an important role by teaching the client to use a problem-solving and goal-setting approach to their difficulties. This method, which is essentially a self-help technique, can be highly effective, especially if the counsellor stays alongside the client as he works through the stages. It enables the client to explore choices perhaps not previously considered, helps him to replace stumbling blocks with stepping stones, and provides the confidence and courage to take risks and implement decisions. And, as an added bonus, once learned, the client has a very useful self-help tool for solving problems that might arise after the counselling relationship ends.

After explaining the process and presenting some examples of goal setting in action, we have provided an exercise for you to practise the techniques for yourself, so make sure you have your pen and notepad at the ready.

What is problem-solving?

Problem-solving resolves a discrepancy. It changes something that is actual, nearer to what is desired. A goal is a result that will reduce that discrepancy. Problem-solving is, in many ways, simply a process of managing information. Indeed, it is probably true to say that in the majority of instances, the only reason we fail to solve problems is that we fail to recognise that we already have sufficient information to do so. Problem-solving has two parts:

1. *Decision-making* which consists of choosing courses of action to reach the desired goal.
2. *Problem analysis* which involves identifying various factors and forces that interfere with or facilitate goal achievement. Planning can only take place when decision-making and problem analysis have been thoroughly carried out.

Identifying the premises of problem-solving

The premises of problem-solving are:

1. To become thoroughly aware of the problem.
2. Problems with one root cause are as rare as two moons in the sky.
3. Effective problem-solving means balancing disturbed forces.
4. Valid decisions depend on accurate, clear and complete information.
5. Working with other people can shorten the process time.
6. People given the responsibility of action must be committed to it.
7. There must be a supportive climate.

Not all counselling is concerned with problem-solving but a great deal of it is. Some people want to increase their self-awareness, to understand a bit better how they interact with others, or to develop more insight of the helping relationship by first-hand experience. Very often the client presents the 'problem' to the counsellor in a jumbled and unclear way. In the early stages, therefore, it is useful to have a plan which counsellor and client can work on together to bring order out of chaos. The model presented here may help. As client and counsellor work through this together, step by step, it will let the client see that there is a logical way of tackling the problem. It will also help the counsellor by relieving some of the anxiety of not knowing where to start.

Identifying the problem

> *A problem clearly stated is a problem half solved.*
>
> Dorothea Brande

1. Establish the problem
   - Identify the origins.
   - Help the client define and describe the problem by using the six key words – Who? What? Why? When? Where? How?
   - Encourage the client to be precise and avoid generalisations.

2. Explore the problem
   - Listen with understanding.
   - Keep an open mind and your questions will be open.
   - Respond with empathy.
   - Concentrate on observable and specific behaviours.

3. Eliminate the problem
   - What is not right about the present scene?
   - What goal does the client want to set?
   - What sub-goals can be set to reach the goal?
   - How can the first goal – then subsequent goals – be reached?
   - Goals must be in specific terms – avoid vague and generalised language.

4. Evaluate
   - Whether the goal has been achieved/partly achieved.
   - Whether the problem has changed.

Summary

The four stages of problem-solving counselling involve:
1. *establishing* the problem
2. *exploring* the problem
3. *eliminating* the problem
4. *evaluation* of the problem-solving process.

Goal setting

One important part of problem-solving that can sometimes be difficult is goal setting – working out a satisfactory solution. Goal setting is a highly cognitive approach which many people have difficulty working with. Goal setting must take into account the affective and behavioural factors as well as the creative potential of the client.

Figure 19 highlights eight important tasks involved in the process of problem-solving and goal setting.

---

1. **Assessment – helps clients identify:**
   ◆ What they feel is OK about their life.
   ◆ What they feel is not OK about their life.
   ◆ The resources they have to draw on.

   Assessment continues throughout the counselling relationship.

2. **Identifying the initial problem**
   Help the client to focus on the initial problem by using Rudyard Kipling's 'six honest serving men and true': What? Why? How? Where? When? Who?

3. **Develop new ways of looking at the problem**
   Looking beyond the now, to what could be.

4. **Goal setting**
   A goal is what a person would like to attain so that the problem can be managed more easily and constructively.

5. **Opening up possibilities**
   There are often several ways in which a problem may be tackled using resources the client may not have recognised.

6. **Making an informed choice**
   Achieving the best 'fit' between resources, personality, and abilities in order to achieve the desired outcome.

7. **Implementing the choice**

8. **Evaluation**

Fig. 19. Eight important tasks involved in the process of problem-solving and goal setting.

Understanding the process of goal setting

To move from:
◆ **point A,** where the client is, to
◆ **point B,** where the client would like to be

counsellor and client need to explore:
◆ feelings
◆ thoughts
◆ behaviours

in order to develop a new perspective and work through hindrances.

Counsellor and client need to work out strategies in order to reach:
◆ **point C,** *getting* to where the client wants to be.

Example

Point A: Where the client is:
Harry is dissatisfied with his job.

Point B: Where the client would like to be:
Harry would like a more satisfying job.

Perspective
Why should Harry stay in a job that does not satisfy?
Hindrances
1. Self-defeating beliefs and attitudes. Harry believes that he could never get through an interview.
2. Misplaced loyalty. Harry has been with the company for ten years, and they have given him time off to take a degree course.
3. The comfort zone is preferred. Changing jobs would probably mean that Harry had to travel further to work, and learning a new job requires effort.

Point C: Getting to where the client wants to be:
One of the strategies Harry decided on was to learn to drive a car, as this would make him more mobile. Harry role-played several interviews in which the counsellor put him under progressive pressure, until Harry felt confident at applying for a new post.

Advantages of goal setting

◆ Focuses attention and action.
◆ Mobilises energy and effort.
◆ Increases patience.
◆ Strategy oriented.

At point A

The counsellor helps clients to:
◆ understand themselves
◆ understand the problem(s)
◆ set goals
◆ take action.

The client's goal is **self-exploration.**
The counsellor's goal is **responding.**

The counsellor helps clients to:
◆ tell their story
◆ focus
◆ develop new insight and new perspectives.

At point B

The counsellor helps clients to:
◆ examine their problems
◆ think how they could be handled differently
◆ develop their powers of imagination
◆ think through: 'How will I know when I have got there?'.

The client's goal is **self-understanding.**
The counsellor's goal is to **integrate understanding.**

The counsellor helps clients to:
◆ create a plan
◆ evaluate the plan
◆ develop choices and commitment to change.

At point C

The client's goal is *action*.

The counsellor's goal is to **facilitate action.**

The counsellor helps clients to:
+ identify and assess action strategies
+ formulate plans
+ implement plans.

Requirements for effective goal setting

Visions, ideas and possibilities all create enthusiasm; behaviour is driven by creating an achievable plan which should have the following criteria:
+ a clearly defined and achievable goal
+ how the goal will be evaluated
+ a realistic timetable for achieving the goal.

Working for commitment

1. Ownership of the plan is essential for it to work.
2. A plan that has appeal encourages commitment.
3. A detailed plan has a logic to it.
4. An effective plan has an emotional content.
5. Flexibility increases the chance of commitment.
6. Clients need to see that the plan is within their capabilities and that they have the personal and external resources.
7. Client commitment is often influenced by counsellor enthusiasm.
8. Getting started by using problem-solving skills.

Brainstorming

Clients can generate a free flow of ideas that might resolve the problem, by brainstorming their thoughts on a sheet of paper. Encourage them to be adventurous by jotting down whatever comes in their heads, no matter how silly it seems.

Case study_____

Jane was having problems at work. Her boss criticised her work constantly, and generally made life very difficult for her. With the help of her counsellor she worked through her feelings about the problem (point A) and then brainstormed ideas of how she might solve the problem (point B) (see Figure 20).

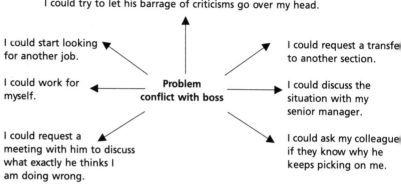

I could try to let his barrage of criticisms go over my head.

I could start looking for another job.

I could work for myself.

I could request a meeting with him to discuss what exactly he thinks I am doing wrong.

Problem conflict with boss

I could request a transfer to another section.

I could discuss the situation with my senior manager.

I could ask my colleagues if they know why he keeps picking on me.

Fig. 20. An example of brainstorming.

The next stage for Jane was to make her mind up which alternative felt right for her, and to plan a realistic goal (point C). She decided that there were two goals she wanted to achieve:
1. To resolve the problems she was having with her boss.
2. To become self-employed.

We return to Jane later to see how she planned her action for reaching her goals.

Force-field analysis

Force-field analysis, a decision-making technique developed from Lewin's Field Theory, is designed to help people understand the various internal and external forces that influence the way they make decisions. It is a way of helping people plan how to move forward towards the desired outcome. For most of the time these forces are in relative balance, but when something disturbs the balance, decisions are more difficult to make. When the forces are identified, counsellor and client work on strategies to help the client reach the desired goal.

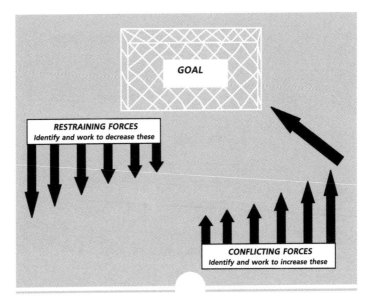

Fig. 21. Force-field analysis.

Stages in force-field analysis

1. What is the **goal** to be achieved?
2. Identifying **restraining forces** that act as **obstacles** to outcomes.
3. Identifying **facilitating forces** that act as **aids** to outcome.
4. Working out how to **weaken** some of the restraining forces, or how to **strengthen** some of the facilitating forces, or both.
5. Using **imagery** to picture moving toward the desired goal and achieving it.

Forces may be **internal** or **external** as shown in Figure 22.

The underlying principle is that by strengthening the facilitating forces and diminishing the restraining forces, a decision will be easier to make, because energy, trapped by the restraining forces, has been released.

Restraining forces

The restraining forces are the obstacles that are, or seem to be, hindering the client from implementing her action plan. Once the restraining forces have been identified, ways of coping with them are discussed. The counsellor must ensure that the client does not dwell on these forces and become demoralised.

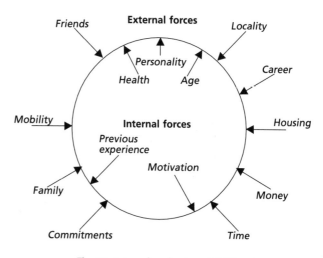

Fig. 22. Internal and external forces.

Facilitating forces

These are the positive forces to be used by the client. They may be other people, places or things. Any factors that facilitate or assist the client to attain her goal are utilised. This part of the process of searching for facilitating forces actually pushes the client to look at her positive attributes.

Everything in force-field analysis should be specific. Imagine you were telling someone how to get from London to Glasgow; you would be as specific as possible. Force-field analysis is a bit like that. You would know you were in Glasgow when you arrived there. Force-field analysis helps the client be specific.

Plan of action

The plan of action is born out of utilising the facilitating forces to reach the defined goal. The plan requires to be simple and easily understood by the client.

Let us return to Jane now to see how she used force-field analysis to identify her restraining and facilitating forces, and to plan her action.

Case study: Jane's force-field analysis in action_____

Goal 1. Jane's identified goal: to resolve the problems with her boss.

Jane's restraining forces: Anxiety about confronting the situation.

Fear of making the situation worse.

Fear of bursting into tears or getting angry.

Fear of hearing something she would rather not hear.

Jane's facilitating forces: Determination.

Dislike of disharmony.

Desire to get to the bottom of the problem.

Jane's plan of action:

1. Prepare a 'script' of what she wants to say to her boss.
2. Ask for a meeting with her boss.
3. Practise her relaxation techniques prior to the meeting.
4. Communicate to her boss how much his criticism is upsetting her, and ask him what exactly she is doing that seems to be causing him concern.
5. Be prepared to compromise to reach a solution.

Goal 2. Jane's identified goal: to become self-employed

Jane's restraining forces: Anxiety about how she will manage for money, until her business is established.

Self doubts about her skills and abilities.

Concern about taking the risk.

Jane's facilitating forces: Self-motivated and works well on her own.

Good organisational and time-management skills.

Enjoys new challenges.

Gets on well with people.

Good communication skills.

Jane's plan of action:

1. Prepare a skills audit.
2. Prepare a business plan.
3. Make appointment with bank manager.
4. Investigate advertising costs.
5. Prepare a marketing strategy.
6. Plan publicity campaign.
7. Inform Tax Office and DSS.
8. Research for potential clients.
9. Plan a start date and go for it!

Coping with complex problems

Complex problems may need the creation of sub-goals, steps towards a larger goal. Each sub-goal has the same requirements as a goal.

Workable plans may flounder on the rocks of:

1. too much detail
2. not taking into account the difficulties some people experience with a cognitive exercise if it does not take feeling, intuition and initiative into account.

There is more to helping than talking and planning. If clients are to live more effectively they *must act.* When they refuse to act, they fail to cope with problems in living or do not exploit opportunities. The attainment of goals cannot be left to chance.

Only when the client speaks of the problem in the past tense has the goal been reached. Many programmes may have to be devised before the final outcome is reached. Clients cannot know whether or not they are making progress if they do not know where they started from or the milestones they should have reached.

Goals should be set neither too low nor too high. Goals set inappropriately high can cause the client to feel inadequate. Goals set too low do not generate enthusiasm.

◆ Goals must be tailored to the uniqueness of the individual client.

◆ Goals that are to be accomplished 'sometime or other' are rarely achieved.

Evaluation

Evaluation should identify:

◆ the different problems and how these were tackled
◆ the goals and how they have been achieved
◆ areas of growth and insight.

Evaluation encourages the growth of both client and counsellor. If counsellor and client are active partners in the evaluation process, they learn from each other. On-going evaluation gives both partners an opportunity to explore their feelings about what is happening and also to appraise constructively what should be done next.

Summary

- ◆ Help the client look beyond the problem and failure, towards success.
- ◆ Help the client construct alternative scenarios.
- ◆ Encourage the client to be specific.
- ◆ Get clients to state goals in terms of definite outcomes.
- ◆ Goals should be specific enough to drive action.
- ◆ Goals must be verifiable and measurable.
- ◆ Goals must be realistic in terms of personal and environmental resources.
- ◆ Goals must be chosen and owned by the client.
- ◆ Goals must be stated in a realistic time frame.
- ◆ Make sure, whenever possible, that the client chooses a preferred scenario from among options.
- ◆ Make sure that the chosen option is spelled out in sufficient detail.
- ◆ Help clients discover incentives or commitment in order to make the new scenario more attractive.
- ◆ Challenge the client to stretch beyond the comfort zone.
- ◆ Help clients identify the resources needed to make the preferred scenario work, including supportive and challenging relationships.
- ◆ The use of contracts enhances commitment.

Exercise

Exercise 18: goal setting

Step 1 – My goal is
Write down a specific goal you would like to achieve within the next few months.

Step 2 – Restraining forces
Identify any obstacles that are getting in the way of you reaching your goal. Include external and internal forces.

Step 3 – Facilitating forces
Identify positive forces that can assist you in reaching your goal.

Step 4 – Restraining forces
Identify ways you can think of to reduce these forces.

Step 5 – Facilitating forces
Identify ways you can think of to increase these forces.

Plan of action

You may find that you do not need all ten steps to complete your plan.

My goal is_____

The steps I need to take to achieve my goal.

1._____
Sub-goal
2._____
Sub-goal
3._____
Sub-goal
4._____
Sub-goal
5._____
Sub-goal
6._____
Sub-goal
7._____
Sub-goal
8._____
Sub-goal
9._____
Sub-goal
10._____
Sub-goal

Evaluation

Step	Goal – action taken	Date achieved
1.	_____	_____
2.	_____	_____
3.	_____	_____
4.	_____	_____
5.	_____	_____
6.	_____	_____
7.	_____	_____
8.	_____	_____
9.	_____	_____
10.	_____	_____

Summary

This chapter has provided you with a goal-setting model that can be used with clients to help them explore and resolve their problems. We have highlighted that, once learned, this valuable tool can be used as a self-help method for problem-solving.

This brings to an end the chapters dealing with counsellor qualities and skills, so it seems an appropriate place to map out what has been covered. (See Figure 23 – an overview of the counselling process.)

Some key points to consider

Before we move on to discuss the topic of preparing for termination of counselling, there are two important points we consider need to be addressed:

◆ It is crucial to bear in mind that every client is a unique individual who comes with their own distinctive set of needs, and no particular approach or model of counselling is right for every client. Don't straitjacket the client, be flexible, listen to the client's needs, and be prepared to adjust your approach if necessary.

◆ In practice, the skills presented in this book often overlap, and it is worth remembering that some clients work more effectively by exploring their feelings – an affective approach

– while others get more from counselling by using their thinking capacity – a cognitive approach. Goal setting is more cognitive than affective; although to be truly effective both head and heart must be used.

Goals are a means to an end, not the ultimate purpose of our lives. They are simply a tool to concentrate our focus and move us in a direction. The only reason we really pursue goals is to cause ourselve to expand and grow. Achieving goals by themselves will never mak us happy in the long term; it's who you become, as you overcome the obstacles necessary to achieve your goals, that can give you the deepest and most long-lasting sense of fulfilment.

Anthony Robbin

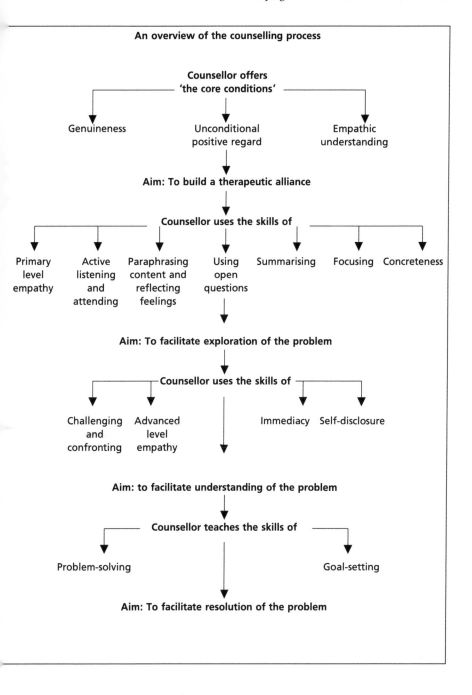

Fig. 23. An overview of the counselling process.

CHAPTER 7

Terminating the Counselling Relationship

The meeting of two personalities is like the contact of two chemical substances; if there is any reaction, both are transformed.

Carl Gustav Jung

Counselling is a relationship with a purpose. Within it are the seeds of the ending that will come when the purpose is completed. Termination is built into the initial contract, and is kept in view throughout the counselling relationship. A 'weaning off' period is recommended, especially if counselling has taken place over a long time.

Preparing for termination

Termination should be well planned and worked through. Premature endings can be very traumatic to both client and counsellor. Termination should be approached with as much sensitivity and caring as any stage in the counselling. When counselling has taken place over a long period, the original reason(s) may have faded into insignificance.

Counselling is like taking a journey; we know where we have come from, and roughly the route taken, but looking back, the starting point has become obscured, partly through distance, but also through time. Unlike a journey, it is necessary for both counsellor and client to look back in order to firmly establish the final position. Looking back to where and why the journey began may prove difficult; feelings, as well as memories, fade with time. Looking back is not always comfortable. It may reveal obstacles not previously recognised.

Terminal evaluation

The relationship between counsellor and client is not an end in itself. Evaluation helps to establish just how the client has been able to transfer the learning into relationships outside of counselling. Evaluation helps the client to realise and acknowledge personal gains. The counsellor, in return, receives something from every counselling relationship.

A terminal evaluation should identify:

1. The different problems and how these were tackled.
2. The goals and how they have been achieved.
3. Areas of growth and insights.

A terminal evaluation gives both client and counsellor a feeling of completeness. It gives the counsellor an opportunity to look at some of those things that did not go according to plan, as well as those that did. A well carried out evaluation not only looks backward, it also looks forward. A final evaluation provides the client with something positive to carry into the future.

Success? Failure? Shared responsibility?

Success is not always so easily measured. A person who comes for one session and leaves saying, 'I feel better for having talked it over, even though there is nothing you can actually do,' may then be more able to cope with life.

For example, Angela, a middle-aged woman, came to see her counsellor, William. She had multiple difficulties arising from a disastrous second marriage. She had left her first husband, 'a boring and uninteresting man', for a 'good looking, jolly, charming man', who later turned into a criminal and who, at the time she met the counsellor, was in prison. She poured out her story, saying as she finished, 'I know there's nothing you can do. But it has helped to talk about it and not hide it.'

Success and progress or failure – whose responsibility is it?

Whose credit or whose responsibility? Unlike the engineer carrying out a bench procedure, the counsellor has no blueprint to follow and ultimately it is the client who must shoulder the responsibility for his own decisions and actions.

> *The counsellor can never remain absolutely neutral or unaffected by the outcome of counselling.*

It would be all too easy when counselling ends without seeing positive results to pass all the responsibility on to the client. If counsellors feel, 'If only I had been more open, more communicative, less defensive,' and so on, this should lead to them fully evaluating their own contribution.

Similarly it may be easy, when counselling ends positively, for counsellors to accept all the credit, forgetting that whatever their contribution has been, it was the clients who were in focus throughout; and whatever was happening within the counsellors, much more was likely to be happening within the clients. If counsellors experience growth from conflict within the counselling relationship, so also will the clients experience conflict and subsequent growth. To the client then must go the credit for whatever success has been achieved. Likewise, lack of success must remain with the client. The counsellor shares in both.

Clients who have succeeded in climbing a few hills are more likely to want to tackle mountains, and, emotionally, are more equipped to do so. Counsellors who have helped create an atmosphere of trust and respect, and have helped a client travel a little way along the road of self-discovery, are entitled to share the success the client feels.

The feeling of failure in counselling is difficult to handle. Blame should not be attributed to either counsellor or client. Both (if possible, if not the counsellor alone) should examine what did happen rather than what did not happen.

> *When counselling goes full term, it is unlikely to have been a failure.*

The feeling of failure, and consequent blame, is more likely when the client terminates counselling prematurely. When counsellors have created a conducive climate, and clients are unable to travel their own road toward self-discovery, then the responsibility for not travelling that road must rest with them.

Travelling at the client's pace

We can only take people along the road of self-discovery who are willing to travel with us. We can only travel at their pace. Unless two (or a group) are in agreement, the journey toward self-discovery will be fraught with impossibilities.

> *The ending of counselling brings the satisfaction of having been involved with the soul of another.*

This is often coupled with the humbling acceptance that perhaps not all that was hoped for has been achieved. Added to this is the knowledge that in the helping, one has been helped; that in sharing the pain of another's wounds, one's own wounds have been touched and transformed. Above all, there is a sense of gratitude that whatever was changed was made possible by both people.

You give but little when you give of your possessions.
It is when you give of yourself that you truly give.

Kahlil Gibran

Counsellors
keep developing
by the guidance
and insights
they receive
from fruitful
supervision.

CHAPTER 8

Getting Support

> When the patient has no hope of his own, he may need to
> borrow some from the therapist to keep himself going. And
> when the therapist is losing hope, he may need to borrow some
> from colleagues.
>
> (Sharon Klayman Farber, 2002:369)

Regular supervision is considered to be an essential element in
the personal development of a counsellor. It ensures that
counsellors work ethically and competently, and serves as a
safeguard for counsellors (and indirectly their clients) should
counsellors experience difficulties in their work, or need to
discuss their concerns about a particular client – for example, a
suicidal client.

What is supervision?

> A good supervisory relationship is the best way we know to ensure
> that we stay open to ourselves and our clients.
>
> (Hawkins and Shohet, 1989:157)

The function of the supervisor is to help counsellors to increase
their skills and develop the understanding of their own and
their clients' feelings in such a way as to increase their
sensitivity and awareness. While this relationship is concerned
with the emotional development of the counsellor, the focus is
not therapy for the counsellor. The counsellor will normally be
in a therapeutic relationship with someone else. Thus the task
of the mentor differs from that of the counsellor, falling
between the polarities of counselling and tutoring.

Increasing your self-understanding

For counselling to be productive counsellors must be

continually moving forward towards increased understanding of themselves in relation to other people.

Time and again they will be brought into contact with clients whose problems will awaken within them something which will create resistance or conflict *within that relationship and specific to it.* The client's difficulty will not be adequately resolved until the counsellor's own resistance or conflict is resolved. It is true that the client may seek help from other sources, but if so, the counsellor's personal development may be retarded. When faced with a situation where our own emotions are thrown into turmoil, or where counselling appears to have reached stalemate, there are three courses of action the counsellor may take. We can pull the blanket over our head and hope that the problem will go away; we can work at it on our own or we can seek help.

In counselling we hope that the client will achieve a degree of insight so that he can see his problem more realistically. If insight is essential for the client, how much more is it essential for the counsellor? If it is necessary for the client to seek help from someone to work through his problem (if he had been able to work it out for himself, surely he would), it is equally important for the counsellor. There is an element of truth in what people say: that one must have experienced something before one can really help others. This does not mean that the counsellor must have been through an identical experience, but it is important that every person who engages in counselling has been the recipient in a helping relationship.

Making the most of the help available

Many people who counsel have personal experience of what it is like to be a client, and it has been this experience that has prompted them to become counsellors.

Not everyone has had this first-hand experience and yet it is possible to experience similar feelings when it becomes necessary to seek the help of a mentor during counselling.

The person in need of counselling has probably put off seeking help and has tried to work it out for himself, but to no avail – the problem is still there. He is bound to feel inadequate; that he should have been able to manage. He may think, 'Can this other person really help?'

The counsellor may experience similar feelings when it is obvious that the counselling relationship has turned sour; that the client is being difficult, resistant, hostile or whatever, or just simply that movement seems to have stopped.

It is no easier for the counsellor in this position to go to someone else for help than it was for the client to approach the counsellor in the first instance. At that stage counsellors, in their heart, come near to knowing how their clients feel. We may resist it and rebel against it, but only if we submit to this experience, when it becomes necessary, will our counselling once more assume accurate empathy.

Understanding the supervisor's role in counselling

Supervisors will assist counsellors to resolve the difficulty that has arisen between themselves and their clients, mainly because the mentor can stand outside and explore with the counsellor what is happening with the client, the counsellor and the relationship between counsellor and client.

The supervisor will be able to use what happens within the supervisory relationship to point to what may be happening between the counsellor and the client. This is similar to the way in which the counsellor may be able to point out to clients that what happens between them may be similar to what happens between the clients and other people.

For the counsellor who has such a supervisory relationship the potential for personal awareness is infinite. Counsellors who choose to disregard such a relationship will lose out and run the risk of eventually becoming ineffective in their counselling.

The essence of the supervisory relationship is simple:

> I proceed with a case of counselling and, on a regular basis, report back to another counsellor with whom I discuss what transpired in the counselling of the client and how the supervisory relationship affects me personally.

Components of the supervisory relationship

◆ To support and encourage the counsellor.
◆ To teach the counsellor to integrate theoretical knowledge and practice.
◆ To assess the maintenance of standards.
◆ To transmit professional values and ethics.
◆ To help the counsellor develop through insight.
◆ To enable the counsellor to develop skills and build self-confidence.
◆ To enable the counsellor to share vulnerabilities, disappointments and to be aware of his limitations.
◆ To help the counsellor move forward with a client if she feels stuck.
◆ To enable the counsellor to evaluate his work and effectiveness.
◆ To share ideas and explore different counselling approaches.
◆ To report on the client's progress or lack of progress.
◆ To recharge the counsellor's batteries.

Three approaches to supervision

1. Focus on the case: characteristics of this approach

a) Exploration of case material.
b) Concentrated mainly on what took place, with little, if any, exploration of the counsellor's feelings.
c) Little exploration of the counselling relationship.
d) A teacher/pupil relationship.
e) Discussion is more in the 'then-and-there', than in the 'here-and-now'.

This approach may create a relationship of the expert and the novice who seeks to please. Because there is often a climate of criticism in this case-centred style of supervision there may be a tendency for the counsellor to skate over the events he is ashamed of or doubtful about revealing – so there may be an 'evasion factor' in the discussion.

2. Focus on the counsellor: characteristics of this approach

a) The counselling relationship and what is happening within the counsellor.
b) Feelings are more readily acknowledged.
c) Carried out in an uncritical atmosphere.

The belief that underpins this approach is that learning is only meaningful if it is personal, so it is advocated that links are made between situations in casework and the counsellor's own personal circumstances. With this approach, the counsellor is likely to feel less criticised and so more supported and thus the ability to learn from the teaching offered may be greater.

3. Focus on the interaction: characteristics of this approach

a) Takes into account both the case and the counselling relationship.
b) The interaction between client and counsellor may, in some way, be reflected in the supervisor relationship. Recognising the interaction, and working with it, is likely to provide the counsellor with invaluable first-hand experience.

The key to this interactive approach is that the counsellor's behaviour with the case is not taken up directly, but is always in relation to what the client might be doing to them. The interactive supervisor knows that the counsellor normally manages his cases thoughtfully and assumes, therefore, what has happened tells him something about the dynamics of the case. Clearly not everything a counsellor does is a reflection of the case, and the supervisor would need to draw attention to how the counsellor is using defences to avoid dealing with a particular issue. Perhaps in certain circumstances he or she might even suggest therapy elsewhere to help, but would not deal with the problem personally.

For details of useful books on supervision see Further Reading.

To effectively communicate, we must realise that we are all different in the way we perceive the world and use this understanding as a guide to our communication with others.

Anthony Robbins

Drawing the threads together

A great deal of work goes into writing a book, and even more in creating a new edition, yet within that there is valuable experience, at least it has been so for us. Counselling is not just learning a technique; it is about one's self. Every client brings new opportunities for self-discovery and self-awareness. The aim of writing a book like this is to share knowledge and experience, to help the reader take one more step along the road toward greater self-awareness. That is why we hope this book has been challenging for you. In counselling we try to hold up a mirror to the client as we do in this book. We hope that you will have been encouraged by what the mirror revealed, that you are a worthwhile person, and that you have a lot to offer other people as you engage in this wonderful relationship called counselling. If anything we have said has challenged you and has led to increased awareness and insight then we are delighted.

Our sincere hope is that this book will inspire you to take your counselling training further, but above all, that you will have travelled a bit further along the never-ending and stimulating road of learning to counsel.

The journey is the reward.

Chinese proverb

Sample Letters, Forms, Checklists and Records

Counsellor's Name
Qualifications

[Counsellor's address]
. . . .
. . . .
. . . .
[Telephone Number]

Date:. . . . .

[Client's name and address]
. . . .
. . . .
. . . .

Dear. . . . .

Further to our telephone conversation today, I confirm your appointment for an assessment interview on. . . . . at. . . . . This appointment will last for one hour, and at the end of the session we will discuss whether you would like to make an ongoing commitment to counselling. To guarantee privacy and confidentiality I should be grateful if you would arrive at the exact time stated above. If you change your mind about keeping the appointment, could you please let me know by no later than. . . . .

As discussed with you on the telephone my fee for the assessment interview will be £. . . . . and my fee for counselling is £. . . . . .per session.

Please find enclosed a map of how to reach my premises (there is plenty of off-street parking available), together with one of my counselling leaflets. I trust the information included in this leaflet is self-explanatory but please do not hesitate to contact me if you have any queries.

I look forward to meeting you on the. . . . .

Yours sincerely

[Signature]

encs.

Fig. 24. Example of an appointment letter.

Counsellor's Name
Qualifications

[Counsellor's address
telephone number]

Date: . . . .
[Doctor's name and address]

Dear Dr. . . . .

Re: Your Patient . . . .
Address. . . . .

Susan attended an assessment interview on . . . . She hoped that I might be able to help with a compulsion to injure herself, which started five years ago, and is causing her a great deal of distress.

I have talked to Susan at length, and have explained to her that I do not feel I have the necessary expertise to deal with this particular problem. I feel she could best be helped by seeing a behavioural psychologist, and should be most grateful if you could arrange this for her as soon as possible.

Susan is in agreement with the course of action I have suggested, and I have given her a copy of this letter.

I am grateful for your assistance.

Yours sincerely
[Signature]

Fig. 25. Example of a referral letter to a GP.

Counsellor's Name
Qualifications

CONFIDENTIAL   [Counsellor's address
                                                telephone number]
Date:.........
[Doctor's name and address]

Dear Dr.........

Re: Your patient .... **Address**.......................

Thank you for your letter dated ...., asking me to see Samantha.

Following your request, I telephoned Samantha, and made arrangements to visit her yesterday at 2.00 pm.

Samantha appeared pleased to see me, and we spent an hour talking about the death of her husband, and the effect it is having on her and Claire. I did not meet Claire, as Samantha's mother had taken her out to the shops.

From what Samantha told me, it seems that Claire is showing very obvious signs of distress because of the death of her father. Samantha, too, is still struggling to come to terms with the death of her husband, and she feels guilty because she cannot give Claire the love and attention she feels she needs and deserves. She desperately wants to comfort her, and to say the right things, but because of her own emotional pain, she is finding it very difficult to cope with her at the moment.

Samantha acknowledged that she needs help and support, and we have therefore arranged to meet on a regular weekly basis. She has decided that she would prefer to come to my office, to give her time and space away from Claire and the home. She feels this will be a positive move for her, as it will enable her to focus on her concerns without any distractions.

We have briefly discussed some of the issues that are causing Samantha particular concern at the moment. These include identifying and understanding the feelings she is experiencing as a result of her husband's premature death, and what she can say and do to comfort and reassure Claire. This will therefore be the focus of our immediate work together.

We have initially contracted to meet for ten sessions, with a view to negotiating further sessions should this be necessary.

Claire has seen a copy of this letter, which I trust is helpful to you.

Yours sincerely
[Signature]

Fig. 26. Example of a follow-up letter to a GP.

Counsellor's Name
Qualifications

CONFIDENTIAL   [Counsellor's address
                                                telephone number]

Date: . . . .
[Doctor's name and address]

Dear Dr. . . . .

Re: Your patient . . . . **Address** . . . .

For the past eleven months Amanda has been attending for counselling once a week. She has been suffering from post-natal depression, following the birth of her son Danny, who is now aged one. Amanda also has a four-year-old daughter called Zoey.

Unfortunately, Amanda's husband walked out on her two months ago, and she does not know his whereabouts. Consequently, she is living on income support, which she is finding extremely difficult.

Although Amanda appears to be coping reasonably well, she is concerned about her children, who are showing signs of missing their father. Zoey has become withdrawn, uncommunicative, and is wetting the bed quite frequently, and Danny is crying a lot, especially at night.

I feel that Amanda and her children could benefit from an appointment with the Child Guidance Clinic, and I should be grateful if you could arrange this for them as soon as possible.

Amanda has given her permission for me to write to you, and has seen a copy of this letter. I have also given her a leaflet detailing the work of the Child Guidance Clinic.

Amanda and I have contracted to meet for a further six sessions, as she wishes to continue working on her own personal issues.

Thank you for your co-operation in this regard.

Yours sincerely
[Signature]

Fig. 27. Example of a referral letter to GP.

Date of initial contact: .... Referred by: ....

Date of first meeting: .... Client's reference:........................

Client's address: ....

.... Post code: ....

Telephone number: Home .... Work: ....

Is it in order to telephone the client at home
or at work if I need to cancel/change an
appointment? Yes/No. Which? ....

Client's age: .... DOB .... Client's occupation: ....

Client's status: Married/Single/Living with partner/Divorced/Separated (Please tick)

Number of children: . . Ages: .... Sex: ....

Client's GP. Name:....................... Address: ....

.... Post code:..................................

Telephone number:...................... Is GP aware of referral: Yes/No

Has client any objections to GP being advised
that she/he is attending for counselling? **Yes/No**

Has client received counselling before? Yes/No

If Yes, who with?..... when?.......... for how long? ....

Reason for termination...

Are there any other agencies involved? Yes/No

Details..

Does the client have any physical complaints? Yes/No

If Yes, what treatment is he/she receiving...

Does the client have any psychiatric complaints? Yes/No

If Yes, what treatment is he/she receiving/has received? ....

Is anybody in the client's family being treated for a psychiatric complaint? Yes/No

Details..

Is the client taking any prescribed medication at the moment? Yes/No

Details..

Does the client take any non-prescribed drugs? Yes/No

Details:...

Fig. 28. Example of an assessment form.

Does the client drink alcohol? Yes/No   If Yes, how many units per week ...

Does the client smoke?   Yes/No   If Yes, how many per day ....

**Does the client drink much
tea or coffee?**   Yes/No   Approximate cups per day ....

**Has the client been involved
with the police at any time?**   Yes/No   Details: ....

....

Presenting problem ....

....

....

....

Family history ....

....

....

....

Life crises ....

....

....

What client hopes to gain from counselling (personal goals) ....

....

....

Length of contract agreed: ....

Fee agreed: £ ....   How is this to be paid? .... Weekly/Monthly/By invoice
                                                                    (Please tick)

If counselling is not appropriate, to whom has the client been referred? ....

Counsellor's additional comments and observations ....

....

....

Fig. 28. Example of an assessment form (continued).

Client's reference: .... Session No. .... Date:.....................................

Issues explored:

....

....

....

....

Counsellor's interventions:

....

....

....

....

Changes since previous session.

....

....

Homework/activities/tasks agreed:

....

....

....

Counsellor's comments about the session:

....

....

....

Matters for raising in supervision:

....

....

....

Date of next session:..................... Counsellor: ....

Fig. 29. Example of a counsellor's case notes form.

Client's reference: ....   Date of presentation: ....

Counselling began: ....   No. of sessions to date: ....

Counselling sessions presented: ....   Supervisor: ....

Points raised in supervision

....

....

....

....

....

....

Comments by supervisor

....

....

....

....

....

....

....

....

....

....

....

Fig. 30. Example of a supervision presentation form.

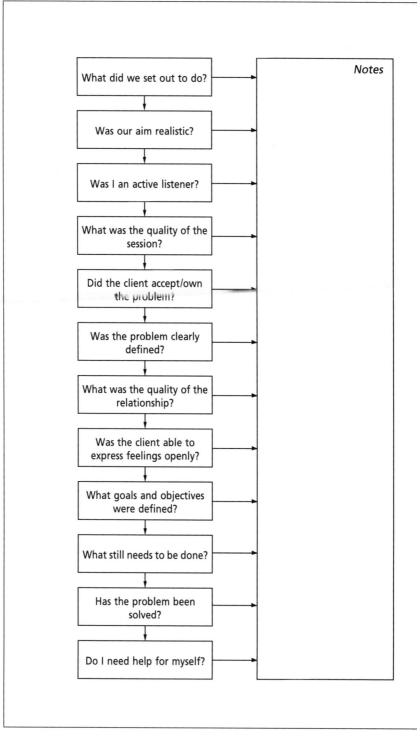

Fig. 31. Counsellor evaluation questionnaire.

1. What happened within me as a counsellor?

	Yes	No
Was I fully attentive to the client?	☐	☐
Was I actively listening to the client?	☐	☐
Did I ask too many questions?	☐	☐
Did I lead the client?	☐	☐
Was I open or closed?	☐	☐
Was I afraid to challenge?	☐	☐
Was my challenging insensitive?	☐	☐
Was I able to empathise with the client?	☐	☐
Was I relaxed?	☐	☐
Was I tense?	☐	☐
Was I friendly?	☐	☐
Was I aloof?	☐	☐
Was I anxious?	☐	☐
Was I at ease?	☐	☐
Was I quiet?	☐	☐
Was I talkative?	☐	☐
Was I interested?	☐	☐
Was I bored?	☐	☐

2. What happened within the client?

Was the client fully responsive?	☐	☐
Was the client responding to me as the counsellor?	☐	☐
Was the client showing evidence of blocking?	☐	☐
Was the client open with his/her feelings?	☐	☐
Was the client prepared to explore?	☐	☐
Was the client waiting for answers?	☐	☐
Was the client an active partner?	☐	☐

3. What happened between me and the client?

Was there participation?	☐	☐
Was there involvement or over-involvement?	☐	☐
Was there argument?	☐	☐
Was there persuasion?	☐	☐
Was there feeling versus intellect?	☐	☐
Was there reassurance versus exploration?	☐	☐
Was there tolerance?	☐	☐
Was there achievement of insight?	☐	☐

Fig. 32. Counsellor session evaluation.

4. Was the following exhibited: If so, by whom?

	Client	Counsellor
Tension release?	☐	☐
Support?	☐	☐
Caring?	☐	☐
Aggression?	☐	☐
Hostility?	☐	☐
Manipulation?	☐	☐
Rejection?	☐	☐

5. Body language and its significance.

	Yes	No
Was there any physical contact between us?	☐	☐

> *Notes*

How did we sit in relation to one another?

> *Notes*

	Yes	No
Did I note any particular gestures?	☐	☐

> *Notes*

	Yes	No
Did I note any particular facial expressions?	☐	☐

> *Notes*

	Yes	No
Was there good eye contact between us?	☐	☐

6. Atmosphere

	Yes	No
Was the atmosphere formal?	☐	☐
Was the atmosphere informal?	☐	☐
Was the atmosphere competitive?	☐	☐
Was the atmosphere co-operative?	☐	☐
Was the atmosphere hostile?	☐	☐
Was the atmosphere inhibited/permissive?	☐	☐
Was the atmosphere harmonious?	☐	☐
Was the atmosphere destructive?	☐	☐

Fig. 32. Counsellor session evaluation (continued).

Date: ....   Client's reference: ....

Counsellor's name: ....   Session number ....

This check list is to help you evaluate your own skills and techniques with your clients. Circle the number that best fits.

5 = Excellent   4 = Above average   3 = Average

2 = Fair   1 = Unsatisfactory

Rate your ability to:

1. Maintain good eye contact with the client   5 4 3 2 1 NOT USED

2. Adopt an appropriate voice tone and posture   5 4 3 2 1 NOT USED

3. Attend to the client   5 4 3 2 1 NOT USED

4. Put your client at ease with you   5 4 3 2 1 NOT USED

5. Accept the client – warts and all   5 4 3 2 1 NOT USED

6. Actively listen to the client   5 4 3 2 1 NOT USED

7. Understand what the client is conveying   5 4 3 2 1 NOT USED

8. Use primary empathy with the client   5 4 3 2 1 NOT USED

9. Feel at ease with the silences   5 4 3 2 1 NOT USED

10. Resist giving advice/offering solutions   5 4 3 2 1 NOT USED

11. Paraphrase content accurately   5 4 3 2 1 NOT USED

12. Reflect the client's feelings accurately   5 4 3 2 1 NOT USED

13. Disclose self appropriately   5 4 3 2 1 NOT USED

14. Use immediacy with the client   5 4 3 2 1 NOT USED

15. Use advanced empathy with the client   5 4 3 2 1 NOT USED

16. Plan action with the client   5 4 3 2 1 NOT USED

Fig. 33. Counsellor self-assessment.

What skills have you felt most comfortable using with the client?

_____

_____

_____

_____

_____

What skills do you need to develop to work more effectively with the client?

_____

_____

_____

_____

What action could you take to develop those particular skills?

_____

_____

_____

_____

_____

Fig. 33. Counsellor self-assessment (continued).

BASIC COUNSELLING SKILLS

Observer .... Counsellor ....

Counsellee .... Date ....

Counselling skill	Highest 1	2	Score 3	4	5	Lowest 6
Attending						
Good listening						
Active listening						
*Reflecting						
*Paraphrasing						
*Summarising						
Empathy						
Silence						
Open questions						
Body language						

Any other comments

_____

_____

_____

_____

_____

Fig. 34. Observer feedback sheet.

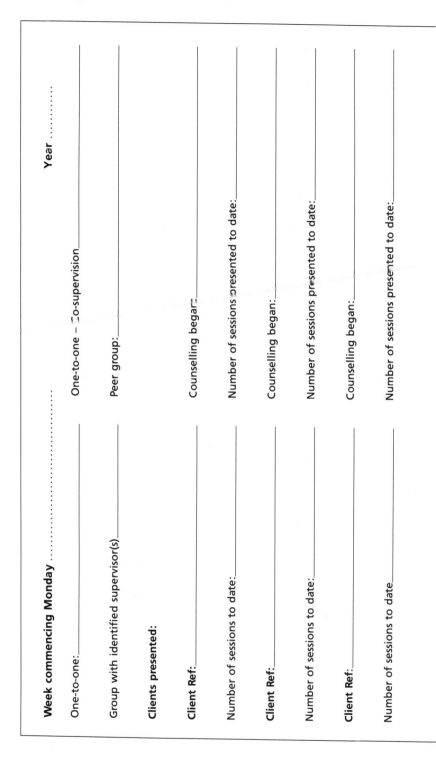

Fig. 35. Supervision hours.

1. **Title of course/workshop**_____

    Date attended: From_____to_____

    Hours: *Theory*_____ *Skills development*_____

    Qualification gained: Yes/No Date certificate received:_____

2. **Title of course/workshop**_____

    Date attended: From_____to_____

    Hours: *Theory*_____ *Skills development*_____

    Qualification gained: Yes/No Date certificate received:_____

3. **Title of course/workshop**_____

    Date attended: From_____to_____

    Hours: *Theory*_____ *Skills development*_____

    Qualification gained: Yes/No Date certificate received:_____

4. **Title of course/workshop**_____

    Date attended: From_____to_____

    Hours: *Theory*_____ *Skills development*_____

    Qualification gained: Yes/No Date certificate received:_____

5. **Title of course/workshop**_____

    Date attended: From_____to_____

    Hours: *Theory*_____ *Skills development*_____

    Qualification gained: Yes/No Date certificate received:_____

Fig. 36. Training courses and workshops attended.

Suggested Responses to Exercises

Chapter 4

Exercise 3 – primary level empathy

Case study 1 – Julie

Feelings: Discouraged, disintegration, drained, frightened, pain, probing, scared, vulnerable.

'You feel drained and frightened because we're getting into some painful areas. What's happening to your friends outside of the group makes it too hot to handle your feelings now, and you'd rather be anywhere than here.'

Case study 2 – Margaret to Keith

Feelings: Appreciation, attention, caring, doubts, expectations, need to prove, pressures, uncertain, worth.

Keith says, 'Margaret, you feel both appreciation and doubt because I don't say the right things, even though, at the same time, you recognise that the way I am.'

Case study 3 – Matthew

Feelings: Able to risk, at home, accepted, confident, edgy, hopeful, open, pretty good, relieved, safe, secure.

'Matthew, you feel both secure within the group yet uncertain, because of your sexuality and how we will respond to you now you've disclosed this about yourself.'

Exercise 4 – correct answers to listening exercise

1. Not listened to   2. Listened to.
3. Listened to.   4. Not listened to.
5. Listened to.   6. Listened to.
7. Not listened to.   8. Listened to.

9. Not listened to.
1. Listened to.
3. Not listened to.
5. Not listened to.
7. Not listened to.
9. Not listened to.
1. Listened to.
3. Listened to.
5. Not listened to.
7. Not listened to.
9. Not listened to.
1. Listened to.
3. Listened to.
5. Listened to.
7. Listened to.
9. Listened to.
1. Listened to.
3. Listened to.
5. Not listened to.

10. Not listened to.
12. Listened to.
14. Listened to.
16. Listened to.
18. Listened to.
20. Listened to.
22. Not listened to.
24. Not listened to.
26. Not listened to.
28. Not listened to.
30. Not listened to.
32. Listened to.
34. Listened to.
36. Listened to.
38. Listened to.
40. Listened to.
42. Listened to.
44. Not listened to.

Exercise 5 – paraphrasing

Case study 1 – Alex

Key words and phrases: have to, cope, own life.

The counsellor says: 'You're saying, Alex, that something is forcing you into making a break from your parents, even though living on your own might not be easy for you, and you're not quite certain you can manage by yourself. You also have difficulty getting your parents to see that you need more independence.'

Case study 2 – James

Key words and phrases: nursing, mates, queers, hard time, really want, what should I do?

The counsellor says: 'Life is not easy at the moment, James. Your mates are ribbing you because you want to become a nurse, yet you're convinced, in spite of what they think about you, that this is the career for you. You would like me to help you make up your mind.'

Exercise 6 – alternative words and phrases

Abandoned	Deserted	Forsaken	Cast out	Neglected
Afraid	Fearful	Anxious	Scared	Terrified
Aimless	Directionless	Purposeless	Goal-less	Pointless
Angry	Furious	Enraged	Bitter	Provoked
Anguished	Agonised	Tormented	Heartbroken	Distraught
Antagonistic	Contentious	Ill-disposed	Opposed	Averse
Anxious	Fretful	Distressed	Overwrought	Troubled
Appreciated	Valued	Understood	Admired	Cherished
Apprehensive	Disquieted	Uneasy	Concerned	Worried
Ashamed	Humiliated	Guilty	Remorseful	Humbled
Bitter	Hostile	Antagonistic	Spiteful	Malicious
Bored	Apathetic	Stale	Weary	Flat
Confused	Mixed up	Baffled	Bewildered	Perplexed
Delighted	Pleased	Triumphant	Cock-a-hoop	Jubilant
Depressed	Dismal	Downcast	Melancholy	Dejected
Devastated	Destroyed	Disconcerted	Demolished	Desolate
Doubtful	Indecisive	Dubious	Sceptical	Uncertain
Energetic	Vigorous	Alive	Overflowing	Active
Envious	Green-eyed	Jealous	Invidious	Malice
Embarrassed	Disconcerted	Abashed	Mortified	Awkward
Empty	Destitute	Bleak	Devoid	Hollow
Exasperated	Irritated	Aggravated	Riled	Annoyed
Excited	Elated	Exhilarated	Stimulated	Inspired
Grief	Sorrow	Heartache	Mournful	Agony
Guilty	Blameworthy	Wicked	Sinful	Wrong
Helpless	Powerless	Defenceless	Unprotected	Impotent
Hopeless	Despairing	Despondent	Giving up	Beaten
Hurt	Injured	Wounded	Aggrieved	Outraged
Inadequate	Defective	Lacking	Incapable	Inferior
Inferior	Poor relation	Second class	Lower	Menial
Lonely	Friendless	Isolated	Solitary	Forlorn
Lost	Bereft	Lonely	Deprived	Empty
Miserable	Sorrowful	Woeful	Wretched	Low
Numb	Stunned	Paralysed	Immobilised	Dazed
Overwhelmed	Swamped	Aghast	Dismayed	Unsettled
Rejected	Excluded	Rebuffed	Cast aside	Dismissed
Sad	Cheerless	Dejected	Dismal	Downcast
Shocked	Traumatised	Disturbed	Numb	Paralysed
Silly	Foolish	Absurd	Stupid	Idiotic
Stifled	Suffocated	Suppressed	Quashed	Smothered
Tense	Edgy	Nervy	Uptight	Uneasy
Tired	Drained	Worn out	Fatigued	Exhausted
Trapped	Ensnared	Cornered	Caught	Tangled
Useless	Worthless	Ineffective	Good-for-nothing	
Vulnerable	Exposed	Sensitive	Defenceless	Weak

Exercise 7 – reflecting feelings

Case study 1 – Mary

Key words and phrases: success, hard work, long hours, suffer, end results.

The counsellor says: 'You're on the ladder of success, and very determined to reach the top. So desperate is your desire to succeed that no matter what it costs, you're going to slave away and, if necessary, burn the midnight oil to get what you want. You fully realise that this stiff climb could be painful and that you may put your relationships at risk, yet so strong is the drive that you won't let anything stand in the way.'

Case study 2 – Sam

Key words and phrases: time, enjoyment, work, chores.

The counsellor says: 'Sam, it seems that no matter what you do, other people always find something else for you to do. It's really bugging you, to the extent that you feel life is just one long chore. You long for some recreation, to have time to enjoy yourself doing what you want for yourself, yet all the time you're being driven into the ground by the pressure from Bill and Susan.'

Exercise 8 – open questions

Case study 1 – Joe

. By the sound of it this has happened to you a few times before, Joe.
. There seems some doubt in your mind that you're in love with Emma.
. It's happened so many times before and you don't really know why.
. You feel fairly sure how you feel, Joe, but not so sure how Emma feels.
. You don't want to end up hurting girls or getting hurt yourself.

Case study 2 – Amanda

. The prospect of going to America doesn't appeal to you.
. You don't like the idea of being separated from Charles.
. There's a fear within you that holds you back.
. Both the money you will earn and being with Charles are equally important.
. Your own work is important to you and Charles's work is important to him.

Exercise 9 – summarising

Case study 1 – Tom

Andy says: 'The last thing you want me to do is to lecture to you like your father did when he was alive. The memory of his constant nagging to do well, and not let the family down, still haunts you, and because you didn't make the grade in his eyes, you feel you let him down, which he never forgave you for. You thought being an only child brought certain privileges perhaps, but instead it has left you feeling pretty worthless and as if you don't fit in.'

Case study 2 – Tom

Andy says: 'You have disclosed some very painful memories and feelings about your parents, and your parentage. There was a lot of venom in your repetition of "bastard" and yet that seemed to unlock some dark and sinister secret that had been eating away at you for years.'

Exercise 10 – focusing

Summarising issues

'Sally, would you mind if I recap? You are sharing a house with four other students, two of whom are untidy and inconsiderate. This is causing arguments and an unhappy atmosphere to live in. You need a car because you live quite a distance from the college, and recently you had a prang in your car. Because you are only covered by third party insurance you have to meet the cost of the repairs yourself, and these are going to prove expensive. The bank is putting pressure on you to pay back past debts, and is already deducting a large chunk of your pay, which is leaving you with very little money to live on. This means that you are not eating properly and are rapidly losing a lot of weight. As if all this isn't enough to cope with, your work is suffering too, and you are now faced with having to resit your last college assignment. You feel completely exhausted and desperate and don't know what to do.'

1. Contrast response
   'Sally, it seems as if things have deteriorated since you moved out of residential accommodation at the hospital, and I'm wondering whether it might be helpful to look at the differences between living in and living out?'

2. Choice-point response
   'Sally, it seems as if there are many issues we could talk about:

- The stress of sharing a house with four students, two of whom are noisy and untidy.
- Needing your car to get to work, and how you are going to pay for the repairs.
- Being in debt with the bank, and being pressed to pay the money back.
- Insufficient money left to feed yourself properly, and losing weight rapidly.
- Having to resit your last assignment when you are feeling so drained and worried because of everything else that's going on. Which one of these issues is the most urgent to explore first?'

- Figure-ground response
'Sally, looking at what we've identified, it seems to me that the most urgent issue is how to balance your account. How would you feel about exploring that first?'

Exercise 11 – being concrete

Case study 1 – Adam

Adam says: 'I don't talk to my wife, except when I want something. When I come in from work I just sit in front of the TV and wait for her to bring my meal on a tray. I do talk a little at bedtime, but usually only when she speaks first. I never ask her how her day has gone. Yet I expect her to have sex with me whenever I want.'

Case study 2 – Judith

Judith says: 'I'm all right if I'm just listening to others, and I really can listen, but when I'm asked for an opinion, or even when I want to give something that I think is important, I just want to curl up and die. I just freeze, I start sweating and my mind might well be a bag of cotton wool. I feel so embarrassed.'

Case study 3 – Bill

Bill says: 'She really winds me up, and how! Whenever she rings me it's "You don't know how lonely I am, Bill, why can't you visit me more often." Whenever she rings off – after pounding my ear for ages – I feel really depressed, yet guilty that I feel like strangling her with the telephone cord, except it's a mobile! I feel really weighed down by her, and even when I am able to get over to see her, it's no better.'

Chapter 5

Exercise 12 – confronting

Case study 1 – Vanessa

The counsellor says: 'Vanessa, you say you want to lose weight, and you realise that your life style probably works against that, yet the way you talk it seems as if you've a "couldn't care less" attitude. Something will turn up, you say, almost as if you're happy that it's out of your control.'

Case study 2 – Dan

The counsellor says: 'Dan I want to challenge you on what you've just said. On the one hand you said you have no problems with your children, and on the othe you said that Bill swore at you. You also said you give them responsibility, yet you refused to respect Bill's responsibility by giving him a key. What do you think about those contradictions?'

Case study 3 – Keith

The officer says: 'You say you don't feel up to handling this change in your life. Yet you are clearly a resourceful chap. You're intelligent and persistent and have coped well with changes in the past. Your Record of Service is first class. Your men speak highly of you, as do the officers. Apart from your coping skills, you relate well to people. I've watched you, and your outgoing personality is one of your assets. Had you considered that?

'Another strength is your loyalty. Your family life is sound, and I know that your family think you're a great guy. One of your other strengths is that you have managed the Mess accounts for four years, so your honesty is above question. Yes, you are scared of such a dramatic change, and maybe you need to think of this as yet another opportunity to show that positive side of yourself in Civvy Street just as you did in Northern Ireland.'

Exercise 14 – advanced empathy

Case study 1 – Nigel to Brenda, a counsellor

Expressed facts:	Likes entertaining. Likes meeting people. Family don't apprec ate his jokes.
Implied facts:	Likes his drink. Is more at home with others than with h family.
Expressed feelings:	Puzzled, hurt, unappreciated.
Implied feelings:	Bewildered, rejected, left out, misunderstood, childish.

renda says: 'Nigel, it seems that you feel hurt by the reaction of your family to your jokes and story-telling. In fact, you get more appreciation at the pub than you do from your family. You've become so used to playing the entertainer that perhaps it's wearing a bit thin for the family who probably have outgrown your humour. Maybe they would rather have you as a husband and father, not a pub entertainer. At the same time, being an entertainer gets you into company with people, but that entertainer doesn't fit too comfortably with the family.'

Case study 2 – Kate, a senior nurse teacher, talking to Simon, a colleague

xpressed facts:	Nurse teacher. Works hard. Twelve years. Her own choosing.
mplied facts:	Lacking enjoyment. Self-imposed. Stressed. Driven.
xpressed feelings:	Regrets, tired, fear, joyless.
mplied feelings:	Trapped, no future, desperation, never getting anywhere, wasted life.

imon says, 'Kate, it seems that you've pushed yourself all these years to get omewhere, and now the driving force has caught up with you. You've put work rst in your life and you've forgotten how to relax and enjoy yourself. There eems to be a desperation in your voice as you think about the immediate future, or you can't see any way out of this feeling of being caught like a helpless mouse n some endless conveyer belt of work and more work, and never seeming to get nywhere.'

Case study 3 – Karen, talking to Joan, one of the counsellors in attendance at the church coffee morning

oan says: 'Karen, what I'm hearing is that on the one hand you say you are ontent with your lot, and on the other I hear a big question mark. For most of ne time what you do satisfies you and it's rewarding, yet within that there are noments of boredom. You say you don't miss going to the office, yet I hear a ertain wistful longing there for change, something to relieve the boredom and outine. It seems as if there's also a certain feeling of "I'm not sure that I should e saying this, perhaps I'm being disloyal". It seems that you may be feeling that ou've reached a stage when you would like to think about something else than ust being a mother and a housewife, something to relieve the staleness, yet just ninking about that somehow feels wrong.'

Case study 4 – Andrea's fourth counselling session with Martin

Martin says: 'Andrea, you feel so totally disillusioned with me and with counselling, that you want to give up. You feel angry that I misunderstand what you say and that I even don't hear what you say. It seems to you that we're caught on a roundabout, getting nowhere. I also hear a desperation that seems all mixed up with hopelessness. Part of you wants to call it a day, yet another part seems to be yelling out quite loudly, "Where else can I go?". I also hear a plea for me to understand you and what you are saying today.'

Exercise 15 – immediacy

Case study 1 – Alan

The facilitator says: 'Alan, I feel a bit uncomfortable in what I'm going to say, as I'm not sure how you'll take it. Over the past few weeks I've become increasingly frustrated and irritated. You are obviously very knowledgeable and have a lot of insight into counselling, and what you say is often to the point. There are times, however, when you've cut across me, as if what you have to say is more important than what I am saying. There are times when the group lapses into silence, as if we're all struggling with some deep issue, and you break the silence with a comment that doesn't seem to be relevant to what is happening. I just need you to know how I feel right now, for it's possible that this is the effect you have on other people. How do you feel about what I've just said?'

Case study 2 – Jenny

'Jenny, I would like you know how I am feeling right now, bloody angry. When you got up and walked out I felt as if you were cutting right across what was happening in the group. Cathy was talking about her pain, something I thought we all felt, certainly I did. I would like to have heard your feelings about what Cathy was saying, for what you have to say is important to me. Yet what you did stopped the action, at least for me, and now I feel angry at what you did. I would like to hear what you think about what I've said.'

Case study 3 – Steve

'Steve, I feel embarrassed talking about money, you probably remember that from our first session, so right now I'm really uncomfortable about saying what I've wanted to for a few weeks. Although you said at the start that the level of fee was OK, several times you've dropped hints that I'm charging too much, and I feel some sort of a heel when you say that. Linked to that is another issue, which is that you say that therapy is taking longer than you thought. I'm wondering if you think I'm holding on to you to increase my bank balance at your expense. How do you feel about what I've said?'

Case study 4 – Sally

'Sally, we've been working together for six months, on and off, and I need you to hear what I have to say. There are many times when we've got along very well, and you've worked hard on this business of getting on with people. At the same time, I often feel I'm being used, particularly when you break appointments without letting me know. I've challenged you several times on that inconsistent behaviour and you've agreed with me. When you agree, I have the impression of a little girl standing in front of the head teacher, with eyes downcast and, at the same time, body shifting very uncomfortably as if you've been caught doing something naughty and that I'm going to punish you. Then you put on that little-girl voice, your eyes open wide and you look as if you're going to cry. When that happens I feel like some monster, so I back off. It's as if you're using that little girl act to score points, and that makes me feel helpless to know what to do. Could we talk about how you see yourself in the mirror I've held up to you?'

Glossary

Acceptance. The feeling of being accepted as we really are, including our strengths and weaknesses, differences of opinions, etc, no matter how unpleasant or uncongenial, without censure. Not judging the client by some set of rules, values, or standards.

Active listening. Accurate and sensitive listening which indicates to the client that the counsellor is truly listening. Includes non-verbal responses such as gestures, body posture, facial expressions and eye contact. Involves listening at a 'head' level to the thinking behind the words, and a 'heart' level to the feelings and emotions behind the words.

Advanced empathy. Works almost exclusively with implied feelings, those that lie below the surface, and hunches. Helps clients see their problems and concerns more clearly and in a context that enables them to move forward.

Advising. Telling other people what they *should* do, rather than enabling them to find their own solutions. To recommend; suggest.

Affect. A subjective emotion or feeling attached to an idea, to some aspect of self, or to some object. Common affects are euphoria, anger, and sadness. Affect may be flat, blunted, inappropriate, labile (shifting).

Affirmation. Positive self-talk. Affirmations are useful for changing a negative self-image to a positive one.

Ambivalence. Simultaneous and contradictory attitudes or feelings (as attraction and repulsion) towards an object, person or action; continual fluctuation between one thing and its opposite, uncertainty as to which approach to follow.

Anxiety. Apprehension, tension or uneasiness from anticipation of danger, the source of which is largely unknown or unrecognised.

Attending. Being physically and emotionally available to the client.

Attitude. A pattern of more or less stable mental views, opinions or interests, established by experience over a period of time. Attitudes are likes and dislikes, affinities or aversion to objects, people, groups, situations and ideas.

Availability. Where we make ourselves emotionally available to another person. It demonstrates our willingness to be involved.

Behaviour therapy. A method of treatment designed to modify observable behaviour and thoughts that relate to behaviour. Aims to help clients alter maladaptive, or self-defeating, behaviour patterns using rewards such as praise, and negative reinforcements, such as withholding attention or disapproval. Also teaches clients strategies for calming the mind and body (relaxation techniques) so they feel better, can think more clearly, and can make effective decisions.

ody language. Non-verbal communication by largely unconscious signals. The principal elements of body language are: gesture, touch, eye contact, facial expression, posture, and non-verbal aspects of speech: tone of voice, volume, etc.

oundaries. The ground rules for counselling. Necessary for the comfort and safety of client and counsellor.

rainstorming. Generating a free flow of thoughts and ideas that might assist with developing new ideas for solving a problem.

atharsis. (from the Greek *katharsis*, to cleanse, purge). A purification or purgation of the emotions (eg pity and fear) primarily through psychology, fantasy or art. A process that brings about spiritual renewal or release from tensions or elimination of a complex by bringing it to consciousness and affording it expression.

hild psychologist. A person who studies the development of the mind of a child.

linical psychology. A branch of psychology concerned with the understanding and application of psychological techniques to a variety of clinical and health problems.

linician. A physician, psychologist or psychiatrist specialised in clinical studies or practice.

o-counselling. A self-directed, peer approach, where two people work together to help each other deal with problematical situations or traumatic experiences. Each person, for an agreed length of time, acts as counsellor to the other, supporting that person while he or she works through the problem and/or expresses their emotional pain.

ognitive Behavioural Therapy. CBT combines two approaches: cognitive therapy and behaviour therapy. This therapy is based on the premise that we are all conditioned by our upbringing to behave and think in certain ways. CBT involves guiding clients through experiences that will change the way they think so that they can change behaviour, and encouraging clients to challenge their negative thought patterns.

oncreteness. Encouraging the client to be concrete or specific about events and feelings, rather than making vague, woolly or generalised statements, and responding in a clear and specific way.

onfidentiality. Maintaining trust with the client by not passing on personal information about them without permission being granted.

onflict. The simultaneous presence of opposing or mutually exclusive impulses, desires or tendencies. Conflict may arise externally or internally.

onfrontation. Anything the counsellor does that invites the client to examine his behaviour and its consequences. Done with sensitivity and caring, it can be a powerful gift to the client and can open up possibilities for change. Pointing out discrepancies to the client, for instance, between what they do and what they say.

Congruence. Agreement, harmony, conformity, consistency.

Contract. Terms on which counselling is offered. Agreement may be written and signed by client and counsellor, or may be verbal.

Control. The need to feel appropriately in control in a relationship, without either feeling the need to dominate or be dominated.

Core conditions. Relationship qualities embraced in most therapies, and considered to be crucial in person-centred therapy.

Defence mechanisms. Unconscious adjustments made, either through action or the avoidance of action, to keep from recognising personal qualities or motives that might lower self-esteem or heighten anxiety.

Delusion. A delusion is a persistent false belief that is both untrue and cannot be shaken by reason or contradictory evidence, and that is inconsistent with the person's knowledge or culture.

Depression. A disorder of mood marked especially by sadness, inactivity, difficulty in thinking and concentration, a significant increase or decrease in appetite and time spent sleeping, feelings of dejection and hopelessness, and sometimes suicidal tendencies. Reactive depression is said to be attributable to a specific event, such as death. Clinical or endogenous depression: both these terms have been replaced by mood disorders, although some people still use them. Clinical depression refers to a depression which is serious enough to need treatment by a doctor. Endogenous means arising from within. In older textbooks the distinction was made between reactive and endogenous, the latter being more serious.

Dialectical Behaviour Therapy (DBT). A treatment method developed by Marsha Linehan, University of Washington, to treat patients displaying features of borderline personality disorder (BPD). Treatment includes: individual therapy, group skills training (comprising four modules – core mindfulness skills, interpersonal effectiveness skills, emotion modulation skills and distress tolerance skills), telephone contact and therapist consultation. The key strategies in DBT are *validation* and *problem solving.*

Eclectic approach. The eclectic counsellor does not adhere to any particular school of therapy or counselling. She or he chooses what is most appropriate from the gamut of therapeutic approaches. The approach chosen takes into consideration the client's individuality and identified needs.

Emotion. A mood, attitude, frame of mind, state of mind, strong feeling, particular mental state or disposition.

Empathic responding. Understanding, or striving to understand, the thoughts, feelings, behaviours and personal meanings from another person's frame of reference, and responding with sensitivity and caring.

Empathy. The ability to step into the inner world of another person and step out of it again, without identifying too closely (becoming) that person. Trying to understand the thoughts, feelings, behaviours and meanings from the other person's frame of reference (to feel *with*, to be *alongside*). Should not be confused with *sympathy* (feeling *like*), or pity (feeling *for*).

Euphoria. An exaggerated feeling of physical and emotional well-being, usually of psychological origin, not attributable to some external event.

Family therapy. Counselling more than one member of a family in the same session. The assumption is that problems in one member of the family affect all other members to some degree, and the interrelationship between family members. Particular attention is paid to the dynamics; how to mobilise the family strengths and resources; how to restructure dysfunctional behaviour. Family therapy should only be carried out by counsellors skilled in working with different family systems.

Feedback. An essential mechanism in any interpersonal communication. It gives one person the opportunity to be open to the perceptions of others. Giving feedback is both a verbal and a non-verbal process where people let others know their perceptions and feelings about their behaviours. Without effective feedback, communication will flounder.

Fight/flight response. The term given to the action of certain hormones within the body which prepares the person to fight or run away from danger.

Flashback. A past incident recurring vividly in the mind, often associated with previous taking of hallucinogenic drugs, but also with traumatic experiences.

Focusing. Helping the client explore a specific area in depth. Focusing helps client and counsellor find out where to start, and in which direction to continue.

Force-field analysis. A decision-making technique developed from Lewin's Field Theory. Designed to help people understand the various internal and external forces that influence the way they make decisions.

Frame of reference. Hearing and responding in such a way that you demonstrate that you are trying to see things through the other person's eyes.

Genuineness. The degree to which the counsellor can be freely and deeply herself with the client. Also referred to as congruence and authenticity.

Gestalt therapy. Gestalt, a German word, does not translate easily into a single English phrase. Loosely, it means: the shape, the pattern, the whole form, the configuration. Gestalt therapy aims to increase a client's awareness of the whole – shape and pattern, and integration of incongruent parts. Gestalt therapists assist clients to work through 'unfinished business' that is interfering with present day functioning by helping them gain insight into what is happening within the self in the here-and-now.

Goal setting. Working out a satisfactory solution. A highly cognitive approach. Takes account of the affective and behavioural factors as well as the creative potential of the client.

Grief therapy. There is no single approach to dealing with grief and bereavement. What people have concentrated on are the various types of grief, and how grief can interfere with normal living. There are various models, such as Kubler Ross and her five phases of grief. A second, and for many, more acceptable, is William Worden's stages model: accept the reality; to experience the pain; to adjust to the new environment; and to withdraw emotional energy from the deceased and re-invest it in new relationships. These are tasks to be worked at.

Humanistic approach. Humanistic psychological, or phenomenological approach to counselling emphasises the uniqueness of each individual. It stresses the subjective experience of the client, rather than trying to fit the client into some predetermined model or theory. Carl Rogers' person-centred approach is probably *the* definitive example of this approach. One of the emphases is self-actualisation.

Hypnotherapy. Hypnosis produces a dream-like or trance-like state. Hypnotherapy is used to help clients achieve specific, short-term goals – reduction, or cessation of, nail biting, bedwetting, smoking, weight, stress levels – relieving pain and depression or overcoming phobias. For many years a controversy has been raging concerning the possibility of hypnotic techniques creating 'false memories' in trauma survivors (memories believed to have been repressed, but in fact are fantasised). These memories (whether real or imagined) can cause considerable distress or retraumatisation. Therefore, hypnosis with trauma survivors should be used with extreme caution, and only administered by a qualified and experienced practitioner.

Immediacy. The skill of discussing your relationship with a client. Also referred to as 'here-and-now', or 'you-me-talk'.

Insight. In psychological terms, the discovery by an individual of the psychological connection between earlier and later events so as to lead to recognition of the roots of a particular conflict of conflicts. A clear or deep perception of a situation.

Integrative approach. Integrative counsellors do not subscribe to one therapeutic approach. The term 'integrative' refers to either the integration of two or more approaches to therapy, or an integration of both therapies and counselling techniques.

Intellectualising. Avoiding gaining psychological insight into an emotional problem by performing an intellectual analysis. Using the *head* rather than the *heart*.

Internal frame of reference. The subjective world of a person. When we view another person within the internal frame of reference, that person's behaviour makes more sense.

Intervention. Intervening with the aim of preventing or altering the result or course of actions.

Judgmentalism. Where we judge people according to our own self-imposed standards and values, and impose them in a way that condemns and criticises.

Mood. A prevailing and sustained emotion or feeling.

Non-judgmental attitude. Suspending own judgments and standards and not imposing them on others.

Non-possessive warmth. An attitude of friendliness towards others.

Open invitation to talk. Demonstrating to the client that you are ready to listen.

Openness. How prepared we are to let other people see beneath the surface; to let them be appropriately aware of our feelings, secrets and innermost thoughts.

Open questions. Keep conversation going and create greater interest and depth. They seek clarification, elaboration and encourage exploration.

Paraphrasing. Restating the client's thoughts and feelings in your own words.

Person-centred approach. This approach emphasises the quality of the counsellor and client relationship. Genuineness, warmth, honesty, unconditional positive regard and empathy are considered essential 'conditions' to a growth-producing climate between client and counsellor.

Pharmacotherapy. Treatment of disease with medicine.

Post-traumatic stress disorder. An anxiety disorder in which exposure to an exceptional mental or physical stressor is followed, sometimes immediately and sometimes not until three months or more after the incident, by persistent re-experiencing of the event, with its associated feelings and behaviours.

Problem-solving. Helping someone, or ourselves, to resolve some difficulty by working to a model or plan, the aim of which is to generate positive action.

Psychiatry. A branch of medicine concerned with the diagnosis and treatment of psychological disorders. A psychiatrist is a doctor of medicine who has received postgraduate training in psychiatry.

Psychoanalysis. A theoretical system of psychology based on the work of Sigmund Freud. Psychoanalysis may be defined as human nature interpreted in terms of conflict. The mind is understood as an expression of conflicting forces – some conscious, the majority unconscious. A deeper and more intense form of treatment than other forms of psychotherapy.

Psychodynamic. The study of human emotions as they influence behaviour. Psychodynamic theory recognises the role of the unconscious, and assumes that behaviour is determined by past experience, genetic endowment and current reality. A psychodynamic counsellor works toward the client achieving insight.

Psychotherapy. Any form of 'talking cure'. The treatment of psychological problems through the use of a variety of theories of personality development, specific techniques and therapeutic aims. Aimed at relieving psychological distress. Psychotherapists use talk and thought, rather than surgery or drugs. May be superficial, deep, interpretive, supportive or suggestive.

Reflecting feelings. Understanding the client's emotional world and mirroring client's emotional content with empathic responses.

Self-awareness. An awareness of our inner experience – what goes on inside our heads – how we think and feel – knowing how we function emotionally. A continuous and evolving process of gathering information about ourselves. A basic need in effective helping.

Self-disclosure. Disclosing personal information, thoughts and feelings to clients. Used to serve the needs of the client, not the needs of the counsellor.

Self-esteem. A confidence and satisfaction in oneself: self-respect, self-worth, self-pride. Self-esteem is the value we place on ourselves. A high self-esteem is a positive value; a low self-esteem results from attaching negative values to ourselves or some part of ourselves.

Stereotyping. Pigeon-holing, putting people into a mould, typecasting, making assumptions – not making allowances for a person's individuality. Stereotyping is typically negative, and is often rooted in prejudice, ignorance or irrational fears.

Stress. An imprecise term, but generally taken to mean a state of psychological tension produced by the kinds of forces or pressures (stressors) that exert force with which the person feels unable to cope. The feeling of just being tired, jittery or ill are subjective sensations of stress.

Summarising. The process of tying together all that has been talked about during part, or all, of the counselling session. It clarifies what has been accomplished and what still needs to be done.

Supervision. Concerned with the emotional development of the counsellor, and developing the counsellor's skills. Focus is not therapy for the counsellor. Supervision falls between the polarities of counselling and tutoring.

Syndrome. A group of signs and symptoms that occur together and characterise a particular abnormality.

Therapeutic alliance. A collaborative relationship between counsellor and client. A strong therapeutic alliance (client-counsellor bond) is considered a necessary condition for effective counselling.

Transactional Analysis. Transactional Analysis (TA) is a system of analysis and therapy developed by Eric Berne (1910-1970) and popularised in his book *Games People Play* (1964). The theory is that we have various ego states, Parent, Adult, and Child (PAC), all of which influence our behaviour. Counsellors using TA work with the client to get more harmony among the three ego states.

rust. Faith in one's own integrity (confidence in oneself), and reliance on the integrity, ability and character of another person (have faith in).

nconditional positive regard. A non-possessive caring, valuing, prizing, acceptance of the client, regardless of how unpleasant the client's behaviour might be.

nconscious. According to Freud and psychoanalysis, the unconscious is that part of the mind or mental functioning which is accessible only rarely to awareness. The aim of psychoanalysis is to bring into the conscious mind what has been repressed into the unconscious. We repress painful memories and wishes, and unacceptable drives. Counselling does not work directly with the unconscious, and that is one of the major differences between counselling and psychoanalysis.

alues. Deeply held principles, standards, or beliefs that we consider good or beneficial to our well-being and which influence our behaviour, thoughts and feelings and how we relate to people.

References

British Association for Counselling and Psychotherapy (BACP), *What is Counselling?* Available online at http:www.bacp.co.uk (13 March 2003).

Gerard Egan, *The Skilled Helper: A Systematic Approach to Effective Helping* (Brooks/Cole Publishing, fourth edition, 1990).

Jan Sutton, *Healing The Hurt Within: Understand and relieve the suffering behind self-destructive behaviour* (How To Books, 1999).

Peter Hawkins and Robin Shohet, *Supervision in the Helping Professions* (Open University Press, 1989).

Philip Burnard, *Know Yourself! Self-awareness Activities for Nurses and other Health Professionals* (Whurr, 1997).

Sharon Klayman Farber, *When the Body is The Target: Self-Harm, Pain, and Traumatic Attachments* (Jason Aronson – softcover edition, 2002).

William Stewart, *Counselling in Nursing: A problem-solving approach* (Harper & Row, 1983).

William Stewart and Angela Martin, *Going for Counselling: Discover the benefits of counselling and which approach is best for you* (How To Books, 1999).

Useful Organisations

The following resources are provided for information purposes and do not necessarily constitute a recommendation. For information on special-rate telephone numbers (08–) or premium-rate numbers (09–) see your BT phone book.

Abuse, rape and self-harm/self-injury services

Association of Child Abuse Lawyers (ACAL), P.O. Box 466, Chorleywood, Rickmansworth, Hertfordshire WD3 5LG.
Tel: (01923) 286888 (10.00 – 1.00 & 2.00 – 4.00 Tuesdays and Thursdays only)
Email: info@childabuselawyers.com
Website: http://www.childabuselawyers.com
Description: Practical support for survivors and professionals working in the field of abuse. Can recommend a solicitor with some understanding of childhood abuse cases, and site contains some useful links and information.

Bristol Crisis Service for Women, PO Box 654, Bristol BS99 1XH
National Helpline (for women): (0117) 925 1119. Contact times: Friday and Saturday nights 9.00 pm – 12.30 am. Sunday evenings 6.00 pm – 9.00 pm.
Email: bcsw@btconnect.com
Website: www.users.zetnet.co.uk/BCSW
Description: A national voluntary organisation that supports women in emotional distress. Particularly helps women who harm themselves (often called self-injury). Provides talks and training courses to professionals, runs and supports self-help groups, and produces information and publications about self-injury.

ChildLine UK
Tel: 0800 1111
Website: www.childline.org.uk
Description: UK's free, 24 hour helpline for children and young people in trouble or danger. The lines can be busy so please keep trying.

Directory and Book Services (DABS), 4 New Hill, Conisbrough, Doncaster, DN12 3HA
Tel/fax: (01709) 860023

Email: books@dabsbooks.co.uk
Website: http://www.dabsbooks.co.uk
Description: Books and information for adults who were abused as children, for
counsellors and workers, and for anyone affected by child abuse.

Kidscape, 2 Grosvenor Gardens, London SW1W 0DH
Tel: (020) 7730 3300 Fax: (020) 7730 7081 Helpline: 08451 205 204
Website: http://www.kidscape.org.uk
Description: Registered charity committed to keeping children safe from harm or
abuse. Kidscape is the only national children's charity which focuses upon
preventative policies – tactics to use before any abuse takes place. Kidscape has
practical, easy to use material for children, parents, teachers, social workers, police
and community workers.

Mothers of Sexually Abused Children (MOSAC), 141 Greenwich High Road,
London SE10 8JA
Helpline: 0800 980 1958
Website: http://www.mosac.org.uk
Description: A voluntary organisation supporting all non abusing parents and
carers whose children have been sexually abused, to provide support, advice,
information and counselling following the discovery of sexual abuse.

NSPCC (National Society for the Prevention of Cruelty to Children), Weston
House, 42 Curtain Road, London EC2A 3NH
Tel: (020) 7825 2500 Fax: 020 7825 2525
Helpline: 0808 800 5000
Website: www.nspcc.org.uk
Description: The UK's leading charity specialising in child protection and the
prevention of cruelty to children.

SAFELINE, King Tom House, 39b, High Street, Warwick CV34 4AX
Tel: 0808 800 5005
Email: safeline@bigfoot.com
Website: http://www.safelinewarwick.co.uk
Description: A voluntary association based in the UK established by people who
were sexually abused as children. Offers counselling, support, a free information
pack, newsletter, lending library, volunteer training and workshops. Website
includes a comprehensive list of links to related sites.

Survivors UK, PO Box 2470, London SW9 6WQ
Helpline: 0845 1221201 Tuesday & Thursday 7.00pm – 10.00pm

mail: info@survivorsuk.org.uk
Website: http://www.survivorsuk.co.uk/
Description: Help and support for men who have been sexually abused or raped. London based. Site contains useful information, links to other sites and a list of accredited counsellors.

The Basement Project, PO Box 5, Abergavenny, South Wales NP7 5XW
Tel: (01873) 856524
Website: http://freespace.virgin.net/basement.project/default.htm
Description: A community resource providing support groups and helpful literature for individuals. Their work has a particular focus on abuse and self-harm. Offer an educational programme for workers which includes training, supervision, consultation, research and publications.

Internet resources

National Association for People Abused in Childhood (NAPAC)
Contains lot of useful information for survivors.
Tel: 0800 085 3330 (Information Line)
http://www.napac.org.uk

Self-injury and related issues (SIARI) (Jan Sutton's site)
Information and support for self-injurers and their supporters. Includes creative works of self-injurers, message board for self-injurers, moderated online support group for helpers, bookstore, articles, and extensive list of resources on self-injury and related issues (self-harm, abuse, eating disorders, ptsd, bpd, dissociative disorders, counselling and therapy).
http://www.siari.co.uk

Survivors of Incest Anonymous (World Service Office)
http://www.siawso.org

Young people and self harm resource
http://www.ncb.org.uk/selfharm

Addiction services

Addiction Recovery Foundation, 122A, Wilton Road, London SW1V 1JZ
Tel: (020) 7233 5333
mail: enquiries@addictiontoday.co.uk

Website: http://www.addictiontoday.co.uk
Description: Publishes *Addiction Today*, the most influential information in the UK
on addiction recovery. Articles include therapeutic techniques, lists of self-help
groups and treatment centres, details of seminars and workshops for professionals
and people in recovery, research, news, complementary medicines, relevant
legislation.

Al-Anon Family Groups UK & Eire, 61 Great Dover Street, London SE1 4YF
Tel: (020) 7403 0888 Fax: (020) 7378 9910
Website: http://www.al-anonuk.org.uk/
Description: Provide understanding, strength and hope to anyone whose life is, or
has been, affected by someone else's drinking.

Alcohol Concern, Waterbridge House, 32-36 Loman Street, London, SE1 0EE
Tel: (020) 7928 7377
E-mail: contact@alcoholconcern.org.uk
Website: http://www.alcoholconcern.org.uk/
Description: National agency on alcohol misuse. Works to reduce the incidence
and costs of alcohol-related harm and to increase the range and quality of service
available to people with alcohol-related problems.

Alcoholics Anonymous, P0 Box 1, Stonebow House, Stonebow, York YO1 7NJ
Tel: (01904) 644026
Website: http://www.alcoholics-anonymous.org.uk
Description: Offers advice and support to alcoholics. In the United Kingdom and
Ireland, look for "Alcoholics Anonymous" in any telephone directory.

European Association for the Treatment of Addiction (EATA), Waterbridge
House, 32–36 Loman Street, London SE1 0EE
Tel: (020) 7922 8753
Email: secretariat@eata.org.uk
Website: http: www.eata.org.uk
Description: A charity working to help ensure people with substance dependencies
get the treatment they need.

Gamblers Anonymous (UK), PO Box 88, London SW10 0EU
Tel: 0870 050 88 80
Website: http://www.gamblersanonymous.org.uk/
Description: A fellowship of men and women who have joined together to do
something about their own gambling problem and to help other compulsive

amblers do the same. Includes a list of helpline numbers.

Narcotics Anonymous (UK), 202 City Road, London EC1V 2PH
Helpline UK: (020) 7730 0009
Email: helpline@ukna.org
Website: http://www.ukna.org
Description: A fellowship of men and women for whom drugs had become a major problem. They meet regularly to help each other stay clean. The only requirement for membership is the desire to stop. Details of meetings throughout the UK.

National Treatment Agency for Substance Misuse 5th Floor, Hannibal House, Elephant and Castle, London SE1 6TE
Tel: (020) 7972 2214
Email: nta.enquiries@nta-nhs.org.uk
Website: http://www.nta.nhs.uk/
Description: The NTA is a special health authority established in 2001, to increase the availability, capacity and effectiveness of treatment for drug misuse in England.

Talk to FRANK (National Drugs Helpline)
Helpline: 0800 77 66 00
Email: frank@talktofrank.com.
Website: www.talktofrank.com
Description: Free confidential drugs information and advice 24 hours a day.

Internet resources
12 Step Cyber Café
http://www.12steps.org
Alcoholism and Addiction Prevention, Treatment and Recovery Resources
http://www.alchemyproject.net/Links/twelve_step.htm
BBC addictions message board
http://www.bbc.co.uk/cgi-perl/h2/h2.cgi?state=view&board=health.10addictions
Drugs.gov.uk (cross-government website to support the National Drugs Strategy and the work of Drug Action Teams)
http://drugs.gov.uk/
DrugScope
The UK's leading independent centre of expertise on drugs. Their aim is to inform policy development and reduce drug-related risk.
http://www.drugscope.org.uk/

Sex Addicts Anonymous: details of meetings in the UK.
http://www.sexaa.org/meetings.htm
The Way Confronting Addiction
Links to organisations offering help with addictions.
http://www.theway.uk.com/links.htm

Adoption services

British Agencies for Adoption and Fostering (BAAF), Skyline House, 200 Union Street, London SE1 0LX
Tel: (020) 7593 2000
Email: mail@baaf.org.uk
Website: http://www.baaf.org.uk
Description: BAAF, based in London and with offices in Wales, Scotland and England, is the leading membership organisation for agencies and individuals concerned with adoption, fostering and work with children and families. They ar also a major publisher, training provider and family finder.

Office of National Statistics: Adopted Children Register, Adoptions Section, General Register Office, Smedley Hydro, Trafalgar Road, Southport PR8 2HH
Tel: (0151) 471 4830
Email: adoptions@ons.gov.uk
Website: http://www.gro.gov.uk/gro/content/adoptions/
Description: The Adopted Children Register is kept by the Registrar General, and contains a record of every person who has been adopted through a court in England or Wales. Website gives information on applying for adoption certificate receiving information on original birth details, and making contact with adopted people and their relatives.

Counselling and psychotherapy services

Association for Family Therapy and Systemic Practice in the UK,
7 Executive Suite, St James Court, Wilderspool Causeway, Warrington, Cheshire WA4 6PS
Tel: (01925) 444414
Email: s.kennedy@aft.org.uk
Website: http://www.aft.org.uk/
Description: Aims to develop the profession and to establish standards for trainin and registration through the UK Council for Psychotherapy.

British Association for Behavioural and Cognitive Psychotherapies (BABCP),
PO Box 9, Accrington, BB5 2GD
Tel: (01254) 875277 Fax: (01254) 239114
Email: babcp@babcp.com
Website: http://www.babcp.org.uk/
Description: A multi-disciplinary interest group for people involved in the practice
and theory of behavioural and cognitive psychotherapy. Produce a range of
publications including pamphlets on anxiety, depression, schizophrenia, PTSD,
general health, OCD, agoraphobia, learning disability, insomnia, chronic fatigue
syndrome, eating disorders, understanding CBT (cognitive behavioural therapy),
sexual dysfunction, chronic pain, conduct disorder and bipolar disorders.

British Association for Counselling and Psychotherapy, BACP House, 35–37
Albert Street, Rugby, Warwickshire CV21 2SG
Tel: 0870 443 5252 Fax: 0870 443 5161
Email: bacp@bacp.co.uk
Website: http://www.bacp.co.uk
Description: The association's aims are to promote understanding and awareness of
counselling throughout society, increase the availability of trained and supervised
counsellors and maintain and raise standards of training and practice. Produces a
range of publications and a quarterly counselling journal. The United Kingdom
Register of Counsellors (UKRC) is part of the British Association for Counselling
and Psychotherapy.

British Association of Psychotherapists (BAP), 37 Mapesbury Road, London
NW2 4HJ
Tel: (020) 8452 9823 Fax: (020) 8452 0310
Email: mail@bap-psychotherapy.org
Website: http://www.bap-psychotherapy.org
Description: Specialises in individual psychoanalytic psychotherapy for adults,
adolescents and children and is one of the foremost psychoanalytic psychotherapy
training organisations in the country.

British Association of Sexual and Relationship Therapists (BASRT),
PO Box 13686, London SW20 9ZH
Tel: (020) 8543 2707
Email: info@basrt.org.uk
Website: http://www.basrt.org.uk/
Description: Promotes the education and training of clinicians and therapists
working in the fields of sexual and couple relationships, sexual dysfunction and

sexual health, and raises public awareness of sexual and relationship therapy.

British Psychological Society (BPS), St Andrews House, 48 Princess Road East, Leicester LE1 7DR
Tel: (0116) 254 9568 Fax: (0116) 247 0787
Email: enquiry@bps.org.uk
Website: http://www.bps.org.uk
Description: Aims: to encourage the development of psychology as a scientific discipline and an applied profession, to raise standards of training and practice in the application of psychology and to raise public awareness of psychology and increase the influence of psychological practice in society.

Institute of Family Therapy, 24-32 Stephenson Way, London NW1 2HX
Tel: (020) 7391 9150 Fax: (020) 7391 9169
Email: clinical@instituteoffamilytherapy.org.uk (clinical department)
Email: training@instituteoffamilytherapy.org.uk (training department)
Website: http://www.instituteoffamilytherapy.org.uk
Description: Provides a range of services for families, couples and other relationship groups, family mediation service, training courses, conferences and workshops.

Relate: The relationship people, Central Office, Herbert Gray College, Little Church Street, Rugby, Warwickshire CV21 3AP
Tel: (01788) 563853 Central Office Personnel Department
Helpline: 0845 130 4010 (calls are charged at local rates)
Email: enquiries@relate.org.uk
Website: http://www.relate.org.uk.
Description: UK's largest and most experienced relationship counselling organisation. Whether you are having problems getting on with your partner, your kids, your siblings or even your boss Relate can help. Local branches can be found by entering a postcode on the site.

The Samaritans, General Office, The Upper Mill, Kingston Road, Ewell, Surrey KT17 2AF
Tel: (020) 8394 8300 (enquiries only)
National numbers: UK 0845 790 90 90
Republic of Ireland: 1850 60 90 90
Email: admin@samaritans.org
Website: www.samaritans.org.uk
Description: Provides confidential and emotional support to any person who is

ıicidal or despairing (24 hour a day service all year round). For details of your
earest branch consult website or your local telephone directory.

nited Kingdom Council for Psychotherapy, 167–169 Great Portland Street,
ondon W1W 5PF
el: (020) 7436 3002 Fax: (020) 7436 3013
mail: ukcp@psychotherapy.org.uk
ebsite: www.psychotherapy.org.uk
escription: Promotes and maintains the profession of psychotherapy and high
andards in the practice of psychotherapy for the benefit of the public,
ıroughout the UK.

estminster Pastoral Foundation Counselling & Psychotherapy,
3 Kensington Square, London W8 5HN
ounselling & Psychotherapy Services
ppointments: (020) 7361 4803/04 (9.00 am - 4.30 pm)
mail: counselling@wpf.org.uk
raining Department
el: (020) 7631 4846 Fax: 020 7631 4819
mail: training@wpf.org.uk
ebsite: http://www.wpf.org.uk/
escription: Exists to extend access to high quality, professional counselling and
sychotherapy and to strive for excellence in the training of counsellors and
sychotherapists. Provides a list of UK affiliate training centres.

istance learning courses in counselling skills and related subjects

ational Extension College, The Michael Young Centre, Purbeck Road,
ambridge CB2 2HN
el: (01223) 400 200 Fax: (01223) 400 399
mail: info@nec.ac.uk
ebsite: http://www.nec.ac.uk/

he Open University, Customer Contact Centre
O Box 724, Milton Keynes MK7 6ZS
el: (01908) 653231 Fax: (01908) 655072
mail: general-enquiries@open.ac.uk
ebsite: http://www.open.ac.uk

he Institute of Counselling, Clinical and Pastoral Counselling, 6 Dixon Street,
lasgow G1 4AX

Tel: (0141) 204 2230
Email: IOfCounsel@aol.com
Website: http://www.collegeofcounselling.com
Description: The College of Counselling is the accredited distance learning college
of the Institute of Counselling. The College offers a wide range of tutor supported
correspondence courses, videos, audio cassettes and books; specialising in
counselling skills training.

Divorce, mediation and lone parent services

Families Need Fathers, 134 Curtain Road, London EC2A 3AR.
Tel: (020) 7613 5060
Helpline: 0870 760 7496 (7.00 pm – 10.00 pm)
Email: fnf@fnf.org.uk
Website: http://www.fnf.org.uk
Description: Provides information and support to parents, including unmarried
parents, of either sex. FNF is chiefly concerned with the problems of maintaining
a child's relationship with both parents during and after family breakdown.

Gingerbread, 7 Sovereign Close, Sovereign Court, London E1W 3HW
Tel: (020) 7488 9300 Fax: (020) 7488 9333
Advice Line & Membership: 0800 018 4318
E-mail: office@gingerbread.org.uk
Website: http://www.gingerbread.org.uk
Description: Provides information about support for lone parent families.

National Council for One Parent Families, 255 Kentish Town Road, London
NW5 2LX.
Tel: (020) 7428 5400 Fax: (020) 7482 4851
Helpline: 0800 018 5026
Email: info@oneparentfamilies.org.uk
Website: http://www.oneparentfamilies.org.uk
Description: Promotes the welfare of lone parents and their children.

National Family Mediation (NFM), Alexander House, Telephone Avenue,
Bristol BS1 4BS
Tel: (0117) 904 2825 Fax: (0117) 904 3331
Email: general@nfm.org.uk
Website: http://www.nfm.u-net.com
Description: NFM is a network of over 60 local not-for-profit Family Mediation

Services in England and Wales offering help to couples, married or unmarried who are in the process of separation and divorce. They are committed to providing mediation to everyone who needs it in all communities.

Eating disorder services

Eating Disorders Association (EDA), 103 Prince of Wales Road, Norwich NR1 1DW
Tel: Admin 0870 770 3256
Adult Helpline: 0845 634 1414. Over 18 years of age. Open 8:30 am – 8:30 pm Monday to Friday, and 1.00 pm – 4.30pm Saturday.
Helpline e-mail service helpmail@edauk.com
Youthline: 0845 634 7650. Up to and including 18 years of age.
Open 4.00 pm – 6.30 pm Monday to Friday, and 1.00 pm – 4.30 pm Saturdays
Youthline e-mail service talkback@edauk.com
Youthline TEXT service 07 977 493 345
Text-phone service for the hard of hearing only: (01603) 753322
Open 8:30am – 8:30pm weekdays.
Recorded Information Service 0906 302 0012 (24 hours, calls cost 50p per minute and the message lasts approximately 8 mins).
Email: info@edauk.com
Website: http://www.edauk.com
Description: Help on all aspects of eating disorders including anorexia nervosa, bulimia nervosa, binge eating disorder and related eating disorders.

The National Centre for Eating Disorders, 54 New Road, Esher, Surrey KT10 9NU
Tel: (01372) 469493
Website: http://www.eating-disorders.org.uk
Description: Effective solutions for eating disorders such as compulsive eating, unsuccessful dieting and bulimia. Counselling, training and information.

The Priory Hospital, Eating Disorder Unit, Priory Lane, Roehampton, London SW15 5JJ
Tel: (020) 8876 8261 Fax: (020) 8876 4015
Email: peter.rowan@priory-hospital.co.uk
Website: http://www.priory-hospital.co.uk/htm
Description: The Eating Disorder Unit consists of 14 bedrooms on three floors. Most of the patients are aged from 14 yrs to 25 yrs old. Although the large majority of patients are female, the unit can also cater for males with eating

disorders. In addition to offering treatment for eating disorders, The Priory Hospital offers treatment for other psychiatric conditions including anxiety, depression and schizophrenia, alcoholism, drug abuse and stress related disorders.

Internet resources

BBC eating disorders message board
http://www.bbc.co.uk/cgi-perl/h2/h2.cgi?state=view&board=health.11eatdisorders

Eating disorder links extensive list of links to organisations and conference transcripts (SIARI Jan Sutton's site)
http://www.siari.co.uk/RS7_Eating-Disorder_Links.htm

UK Treatment Facilities (Something Fishy Site)
http://www.something-fishy.org/treatment/uk.php

Fertility services

British Fertility Society, 22 Apex Court, Woodlands, Bradley Stoke, Bristol BS32 4JT
Tel: (01454) 642217 Fax: (01454) 642222
Email: bfs@bioscientifica.com
Website: http://www.britishfertilitysociety.org.uk
Description: A national multidisciplinary organisation representing professionals practising in the field of reproductive medicine. Its members include gynaecologists, research scientists, counsellors, nurses, embryologists, andrologists and urological surgeons.

Infertility Network UK, Charter House, 43 St Leonards Road, Bexhill on Sea, East Sussex TN40 1JA
Advice line: 0870 118 80 88
Website: http://www.infertilitynetworkuk.com/
Description: Aims to help all those affected by fertility problems.

Loss and bereavement services

Child Death Helpline
Tel: 0800 282 986 (Open 365 days a year. Every evening 7.00 pm – 10.00 pm, Monday to Friday 10.00 am – 1.00 pm, and Wednesday afternoon 1.00 pm – 4.00 pm)
Website: http://www.childdeathhelpline.org.uk

Description: A Helpline for all those affected by the death of a child. Provides local contacts.

Cruse Bereavement Care, Cruse House, 126 Sheen Road, Richmond, Surrey TW9 1UR
Tel: (020) 8939 9530 Fax (020) 8940 7638
Helpline: 0870 167 1677
Email: helpline@crusebereavementcare.org.uk
Website: www.crusebereavementcare.org.uk
Description: Offers help and counselling for bereaved people as well as a range of useful publications.

Foundation for the Study of Infant Deaths, Artillery House, 11–19 Artillery Row, London SW1P 1RT
Tel: 0870 787 0885 (general enquiries)
Helpline: 0870 787 0554
Email: fsid@sids.org.uk
Website: http://www.sids.org.uk/fsid
Description: Aims to prevent unexpected infant death and promote baby health. Offers a range of support leaflets for bereaved families. Also produces a series of leaflets, books, posters, fact files and videos for parents, students, carers, health professionals and anyone interested in knowing more about cot death.

Miscarriage Association, Head Office, c/o Clayton Hospital, Northgate, Wakefield, West Yorkshire WF1 3JS
Tel: (01924) 200795 (admin)
Helpline: (01924) 200799
Scottish helpline: (0131) 334 8883
Email: info@miscarriageassociation.org.uk
Website: http://www.miscarriageassociation.org.uk/
Description: Offers support to those who have suffered the loss of a baby in pregnancy. Has 50 support groups across the UK, where people can meet and share their experiences and feelings. Produces leaflets, factsheets and audiotapes and works to raise awareness and sensitivity amongst health care professionals through lectures, workshops and articles in professional journals. Site contains a useful list of links to related sites.

SANDS (Stillbirth and Neonatal Death Society), 28 Portland Place, London W1B 1LY
Tel: (020) 7436 7940 Fax: (020) 7436 3715
Helpline: (020) 7436 5881 (10:00 am – 3.00 pm Monday to Friday).

Email: support@uk-sands.org
Website: http://www.uk-sands.org/
Description: Provides support for parents and families whose baby is stillborn or
dies soon after birth.

The Compassionate Friends for Bereaved Parents, 53 North Street, Bristol
BS3 IEN
Tel: 0845 120 37 85
Helpline: 0845 123 23 04
Email: Information and Support: info@tcf.org.uk
Website: http://www.tcf.org.uk
Description: Offers understanding, support and encouragement to others after the
death of a child or children.

Mental health services

Association for Post Natal Illness, 145 Dawes Road, Fulham, London
SW6 7EB
Helpline: (020) 7386 0868 Fax: (020) 7386 8885
Email: info@apni.org
Website: http://www.apni.org
Description: Provides support to mothers suffering from post-natal illness. Aims to
raise public awareness of the illness and to encourage research into its cause.

Depression Alliance, 35 Westminster Bridge Road, London SE1 7JB
Tel: 0845 123 23 20
Website: http://www.depressionalliance.org
Description: Leading UK charity for people affected by depression. Works to
relieve and to prevent depression by providing information, support and
understanding. They also campaign to raise awareness amongst the general public
about the realities of depression.

Fellowship of Depressives Anonymous, Box FDA, Ormiston House, 32–36 Pellam
Street, Nottingham NG1 2EG
Tel: 0870 774 4320 (Information line) Fax: 0870 774 4319
Website: www.depressionanon.co.uk
Description: FDA is a UK nationwide self-help organisation made up of individual
members and groups which meet locally on a regular basis for mutual support.

Manic Depression Fellowship, Castle Works, 21 St. George's Road,
London SE1 6ES
Tel: (020) 7793 2600 Fax: (020) 7793 2639
Email: mdf@mdf.org.uk
Website: http://www.mdf.org.uk
Description: The Manic Depression Fellowship works to enable people affected by
manic depression to take control of their lives.

Mind, 15–19 Broadway, London E15 4BQ
Tel: (020) 8519 2122 Fax: (020) 8522 1725
MindinfoLine: 0845 766 0163
Email: contact@mind.org.uk
Website: http://www.mind.org.uk
Description: Mind is the leading mental health charity in England and Wales. They
work to create a better life for everyone with experience of mental distress. Also
publishes a wide range of books, factsheets, booklets and reports.

The ME Association, 4 Top Angel, Buckingham Industrial Park, Buckingham
MK18 1TH
Tel: 0871 222 7824 (Information line) Fax: (01280) 821602
E-mail: meconnect@meassociation.org.uk
Website: http://www.meassociation.org.uk
Description: Informing and supporting those affected by Myalgic Encephalopathy,
Chronic Fatigue Syndrome & Post-Viral Fatigue Syndrome.

The Mental Health Foundation, 83 Victoria Street, London SW1H 0HW
Tel: (020) 7802 0300 Fax: (020) 7802 0301
Email: mhf@mhf.org.uk
Website: http://www.mentalhealth.org.uk/
Description: Comprehensive website on mental health (and mental illness). Carries
out vital work in supporting people with mental health problems. Information on
a wide range of specific mental health issues from attention deficit disorder to
obsessive compulsive disorders to eating disorders to stress to self-harm, etc.

Senior citizens

Age Concern England, Astral House, 1268 London Road, London SW16 4ER
Tel: (020) 8765 7200
Tel: 0800 00 99 66 (Information Line)
Email: ace@ace.org.uk
Website: http://www.ageconcern.org.uk

Description: Provides a wide range of information on issues such as money, legal topics, health, community care, housing, transport, heating, and leisure and education. Also campaigns and researches age-related issues. Local groups throughout UK.

Help the Aged, Head Office, 207–221 Pentonville Road, London N1 9UZ
Tel: (020) 7278 1114
Email: info@helptheaged.org.uk
Website: http://www.helptheaged.org.uk
Description: Provides a range of services to help older people live independent lives, particularly those who are frail, isolated, or poor.

Internet resources

Action on Elder Abuse
Helpline: 0808 808 8141
http://www.elderabuse.org.uk

Seniors' Health (List of links from Patient UK)
http://www.patient.co.uk/seniors_health.htm

Victims of crime

Victim Support, National Office, Cranmer House, 39 Brixton Road, London SW9 6DZ
Tel. (020) 7735 9166
Victim Supportline: 0845 30 30 900.
Email: contact@victimsupport.org.uk
Website: http://www.victimsupport.org/
Description: Victim Support is committed to providing people affected by crime with support and information to help them cope with their experience.

Useful Internet Resources

Author websites and pages

Jan Sutton

Self-injury and related issues (SIARI)
Information and support for self-injurers and their supporters. Includes creative works of self-injurers, message board for self-injurers, moderated online support group for helpers, bookstore, articles, and extensive list of resources on self-injury and related issues (self-harm, abuse, eating disorders, ptsd, bpd, dissociative disorders, counselling and therapy).
http://www.siari.co.uk

Self-injury, abuse and trauma directory
A unique one-stop listing of self-injury, abuse and trauma resources on the web. Frequently updated.
http://www.self-injury-abuse-trauma-directory.info

William Stewart

Personal Page (includes excerpts and details of William's books)
http://www.author-fellowship.co.uk/willstew.htm

Carl Rogers

A comprehensive bibliography of Carl Rogers' work compiled by Peter Schmid.
http://members.1012surfnet.at/pfs/bibliocrr0.htm

Biography of Carl Rogers written by his daughter Natalie Rogers
http://www.nrogers.com/carlrogersbio.html
Links to The Carl Rogers archives and books
http://www.nrogers.com/carlrogerslinks.html

Client/person-centred counselling/therapy

A wide collection of Person/Client-Centred material by Allan Turner. Associations, books, directory of counsellors, training, papers, videos, links etc.
http://www.allanturner.co.uk

Articles

Instructions for Beginning to Practice Client-Centered Therapy, Barbara Temaner Brodley, Ph.D. Illinois School of Professional Psychology, Chicago
http://world.std.com/~mbr2/cct.beginning.practise.html

Natalie Rogers Website
http://www.nrogers.com

The Development of Nondirective Therapy, Nathaniel J. Raskin
University of Chicago. Originally published in the *Journal of Consulting Psychology*, 1948, 12, 92-110
http://world.std.com/~mbr2/cct.development.html

Codes of ethics and practice

American Counseling Association: Code of Ethics and Standards of Practice
http://www.counseling.org/resources/ethics.htm

Association of Christian Counsellors (UK): Code of ethics and practice for counsellors
http://website.lineone.net/~accord/ACC_Code_Of_Ethics.htm

British Association for Counselling and Psychotherapy: Ethical framework for good practice in counselling and psychotherapy
http://www.bacp.co.uk/ethical_framework/

Counsellor training

BACP: Training, accreditation and details of accredited courses
http://www.bacp.co.uk/education/training.html

Relate: Training to be a counsellor with Relate
http://www.relate.org.uk/workforrelate/becomeacounsellor/

Dictionaries, directories and databases (health related)

Antidepressant drug database
http://www.coreynahman.com/antidepressantdrugsdatabase.html

Online dictionary of mental health
http://www.human-nature.com/odmh

Online medical dictionary (*Cancer*WEB.uk)
http://cancerweb.ncl.ac.uk/cgi-bin/omd?query=&action=Home

Patient UK: A directory of health, disease, and related websites edited by two GPs.
http://www.patient.co.uk

MedicineNet medical terms dictionary (US site)
http://www.medicinenet.com/script/main/AlphaIdx.asp?li=MNI&p=A_DICT

RX List the internet drug index
http://www.rxlist.com

Health and mental health

NetDoctor (UK's independent health website)
Contains a wealth of useful information on diseases and conditions, medicines, depression and much more.
http://www.netdoctor.co.uk

The Royal College of Psychiatrists' Website
Online mental health resource. Invaluable resource includes free fact sheets on a wide range of mental health issues.
http://www.rcpsych.ac.uk

Internet counselling, therapy and resources

4therapy.com: A wealth of useful information and resources
http://www.4therapy.com/consumer

ABC's of Internet Therapy
http://www.metanoia.org/imhs

Association for the Development of the Person-Centered Approach
http://www.adpca.org

Association for psychoanalytic psychotherapy in the National Health Service
http://www.app-nhs.org.uk/

BAPCA (British association for the Person-Centred Approach)
http://www.bapca.org.uk/

British Association of Social Workers
http://www.basw.co.uk

British Psychological Society
http://www.bps.org.uk

Co-Counselling International (UK)
http://www.shef.ac.uk/cci

Connections Christian Counselling
http://www.christian.connections-c.com

Counselling and Therapy Links (edited by Jan Sutton)
http://www.siari.co.uk/RS11-CounsellingandTherapy-Links.htm

Counselling in Primary Care Trust
http://www.cpct.co.uk

Hampshire Association for Counselling: Resource directory of counsellors in and around Hampshire.
http://www.haoc.btinternet.co.uk/choice.htm

Internet therapy and self help groups the pros and cons.
http://webpages.charter.net/stormking/Chapter5/selfhelp.html

Institute of Transactional Analysis
http://www.ita.org.uk

London Marriage Guidance Website
http://www.londonmarriageguidance.org.uk

List of abbreviations (Hampshire Association for Counselling)
http://www.haoc.btinternet.co.uk/abbreviations.htm

Phone advice: Patient UK Healthline and other helplines including a list of telephone advice lines of some national organisations, and a link to the Telephone Helplines Association
http://www.patient.co.uk/phone.htm

Professional counselling resources. Includes links to many UK and international counselling and psychotherapy organisations.
http://www.support4learning.org.uk/counsel/prof.htm

Recovery Resources for Alcoholism, Addiction and Mental Health
http://soberrecovery.com/links/counselingandtherapy.html

Seeking a Therapist
http://www.bacp.co.uk/seeking_counsellor/seeking_counsellor_frameset2.htm

The ethics and law of online therapy
http://www.newtherapist.com/ethicsonline.html

therapyindex.com: online counselling and psychotherapy resource. Comprehensive details of practitioners worldwide
http://www.therapyindex.com/home.php

Therapy UK: List of UK counsellors and therapists.
http://www.therapyuk.co.uk

UK Council for Psychotherapy
http://www.psychotherapy.org.uk

UK Resource Database of Therapeutic Practitioners
http://www.therapistuk.com/therapeutic_resource.htm

UKtherapist.com: Directories for finding psychotherapists, counsellors, and complementary practitioners
http://www.uktherapists.com/

Online bookshops and sites specialising in counselling, therapy and mental health books

BACP: Publications
http://www.bacp.co.uk/publications/

Counsellingbooks.com (working in conjunction with BACP)
http://www.counsellingbooks.com

Counselling and Counsellor Supervision Books
http://123counselling.com/books

Counselling Literature
www.psychohelp.co.uk

Relate Bookshop
http://www.relate.org.uk/RelateBooks.asp

Smallwood Publishing Group: Resources for Mental Health and Education Professionals
http://www.smallwood.co.uk

Further Reading

A Beginner's Guide to Training in Counselling and Psychotherapy, Robert Bor and Stephen Palmer (eds) (Sage Publications, 2001).

An Introduction to Counselling, John McLeod (Open University Press, 1998, 2nd edn).

A-Z of Counselling Theory and Practice, William Stewart (Nelson Thornes, 2001, 3rd edn).

Basic Skills in Psychotherapy and Counseling, Christiane Brems (Wadsworth, 2000).

Becoming a Therapist, Malcolm C. Cross and Linda Papadopoulos (Brunner-Routledge, 2001).

Beyond Empathy, Richard G. Erskine, Jane Moursand and Rebecca Trautmann (Brunner/Mazel, 1999).

Brief Counselling: A practical guide for beginning practitioners, Windy Dryden and Colin Feltham (Open University Press, 1992).

Carl Rogers, Brian Thorne (Sage Publications, 1992).

Case Material and Role Play in Counselling Training, Janet Tolan and Susan Lendrum (Routledge, 1995).

Client Assessment, Stephen Palmer and Gladeana McMahon (eds) (Sage Publications, 1997).

Client Centred Therapy, Carl Rogers, (Constable, 1976, new edition).

Contracts in Counselling, Charlotte Sills (ed) (Sage Publications, 1997).

Counselling Adolescents, David Geldard and Kathryn Geldard (Sage Publications, 1999).

Counselling Children, Kathryn Geldard and David Geldard (Sage Publications, 1997).

Counselling for Toads, Robert De Board (Routledge, 1997).

Counselling in Careers Guidance, Migel Jayasinghe (Open University Press, 2001).

Counselling in General Practice, Roslyn Corney and Rachel Jenkins (eds) (Routledge, 1992).

Counselling in Independent Practice, Gabrielle Syme (Open University Press, 1994).

Counselling Skills and Theory, Margaret Hough (Hodder & Stoughton, 1998).

Counselling Skills for Health Professionals, Philip Burnard (Nelson Thornes, 1999, 3rd edn).

Counselling Skills for Nurses, V. Tschudin (ed) (Bailliere Tindall, 1995, 4th edn).

Counselling Skills for Teachers, Gail King (Open University Press, 1999).

Counselling Skills in Palliative Care, John Davy and Susan Ellis (Open University Press, 2000).

Counselling Skills in Social Work Practice, Janet Seden (Open University Press, 1999).

Counselling Skills, Francesca Inskipp (National Extension College, 1997, 2nd rev edn).

Counselling, Psychotherapy and the Law, Peter Jenkins (Sage Publications, 1997).

Counselling: The skills of problem-solving, Anne Munro, Bob Manthei, John Small (Routledge, 1991).

Counselling: the Trainer's Handbook, Francesca Inskipp (National Extension College, 1993, rev. edn).

Developing Counselling Skills in the Workplace, Di Kamp (McGraw-Hill, 1996).

Developing Person-centred Counselling, Dave Mearns (Sage Publications, 1994).

Essential Counselling and Therapy Skill, Richard Nelson-Jones (Sage Publications, 2002)

Exercises in Helping Skills, Gerard Egan (Brooks Cole, 1998, 6th edn).

Experiences of Person-centred Counselling Training, Laura Buchanan (PCCS Books, 2000).

First Steps in Counselling, Peter Sanders (PCCS Books, 1996, 2nd edn).

First Steps in Counselling, Ursula O'Farrell (Veritas Publications, 1999, 2nd edn).

Going for Counselling: Discover the benefits of counselling and which approach is best for you, William Stewart and Angela Martin (How To Books, 1999).

Handbook of Individual Therapy, Windy Dryden (ed) (Sage Publications, 1996).

Introduction to Counselling and Psychotherapy, Stephen Imer and Stephen Palmer (eds) (Sage Publications, 1999).

Introduction to Counselling Skills, Richard Nelson-Jones (Sage Publications, 1999).

Introduction to Counselling Theory, Jean Bayliss (National Extension College, 1996).

Introduction to Multicultural Counseling, Wanda M. L. Lee (Accelerated Development, 1999).

Introduction to the Counseling Profession, Dave Capuzzi (ed), Douglas Gross, David Capuzzi, Douglas R. Gross (Allyn & Bacon, 2000).

Introduction to Therapeutic Counseling, Jeffrey Kottler, Robert Brown (Wadsworth, 1999, 4th edn).

Key Issues for Counselling in Action, Windy Dryden (ed) (Sage Publications, 1988).

Know Yourself! Self-awareness Activities for Nurses and other Health Professionals, Philip Burnard (Whurr, 1997).

Learning and Being in Person-centred Counselling, Tony Merry (PCCS Books,

1999).

earning and Writing in Counselling, Mhairi MacMillan and Dot Clark (Sage
  Publications, 1998).

istening Helpfully, Jeanne Ellin (Souvenir Press, 1994).

1edical and Psychiatric Issues for Counsellors, Brian Daines, Linda Gask and Tim
  Usherwood (Sage Publications, 1997).

)n Becoming a Counsellor, Eugene Kennedy and Sara. C. Charles (Newleaf, 2002,
  rev. and updated edn).

)n Becoming a Person, Carl Rogers (Constable, 1977, new edn).

)n Being a Client, David Howe (Sage Publications, 1993).

'erson-centred Counselling and Christian Spirituality, Brian Thorne (Whurr,1998).

'erson-centred Counselling in Action, Dave Mearns & Brian Thorne (Sage
  Publications, 1999).

'erson-centred Counselling Training, Dave Mearns (Sage Publications, 1997).

'erson-centred Therapy Today: New Frontiers in Theory and Practice, Dave Mearns
  and Brian Thorne (Sage Publications, 2000).

'ractical Counselling and Helping Skills, Richard Nelson-Jones (Continuum
  International Publishing Group, 2000, 4th edn).

'ractical Counselling and Helping, Philip Burnard (Routledge, 1999).

'rocess Work in Person-centred Therapy, Richard Worsley (Palgrave Macmillan,
  2001).

)uestions and Answers on Counselling in Action, Windy Dryden (ed) (Sage
  Publications, 1993).

elf-Counselling: How to develop the skills to positively manage your life, William
  Stewart (How To Books, 1998).

tandards and Ethics for Counselling in Action, Tim Bond (Sage Publications, 2000,
  2nd edn).

he Carl Rogers Reader, Howard Kirschenbaum and Valerie Land Henderson (eds)
  (Constable, 1990).

he Counsellor's Handbook, Rowan Bayne, Ian Horton, Tony Merry, Elizabeth
  Noyes and Gladeana McMahon (Nelson Thornes, 1999, 2nd edn).

he First Helping Interview: Engaging the Client and Building Trust, Sara F. Fine
  and Paul H. Glasser (Sage Publications, 1996).

he Skilled Helper, Gerard Egan (Wadsworth, 2001, 7th edn).

he Therapeutic Use of Self, Val Wosket (Routledge, 1999).

ime-limited Therapy in a General Practice Setting, Glyn Hudson-Allez (Sage
  Publications, 1997).

Supervision

Counselling Supervision in Context, Michael Carroll and Elizabeth Holloway (eds) (Sage Publications, 1998).

In Search of Supervision, Michael Jacobs (ed) (Open University Press, 1996).

Supervision and Counselling, Gaie Houston (Rochester Foundation, 2nd rev edn, 1995).

Supervision in the Helping Professions, Peter Hawkins and Robin Shohet (eds) (Open University Press, 2000).

Supervising the Counsellor, Steve Page and Val Wosket (Brunner-Routledge, 2001)

Index